MANAGEMENT/ MISMANAGEMENT STYLES

How to Identify a Style and What To Do About It

by
Ichak Kalderon Adizes, Ph.D.
Director of Professional Services and CEO of
The Adizes Institute

Library of Congress Cataloging-in-Publication Data

Adizes, Ichak.
 Management/Mismanagement Styles: how to identify a style and what to do about it

Library of Congress Control Number: 2003097620

ISBN: 0-937120-01-4

Published by:
The Adizes Institute Publishing
2815 East Valley Road
Santa Barbara, CA, 93108,
805-565-2901
www.adizes.com

Printed in China

This book is dedicated to the memory of:

My grandparents: Mushon and Gentil Kalderon;
My uncles: Haim, Rahamim, and Yosef Kalderon;
My aunts: Hermosa, Hana and Lea;
My first cousins: Bela, Matika, Stela, Yoshko, Mosho (age 13)–and
Ketica (age 8);

who perished in the ovens of Treblinka.

On the 60th anniversary of their deportation to the camp.

Acknowledgements

I want to thank Nan Goldberg who has diligently edited this book into a readable form and put up with my endless rewritings. Without her this book would not see the light of the day.

Zvonko Kuzmanovski labored on publishing this book and organized all that is needed for making it happen.

Martha Bright checked the spelling and did the copy editing.

Thank you all.

About the Author

Dr. Ichak Adizes is one of the world's leading experts in improving the performance of businesses and governments by making fundamental changes without the chaos and destructive conflict that plague many change efforts. Over the past 35 years, Dr. Ichak Adizes has worked with some of the largest commercial organizations in the world and has consulted to many heads of state. The methodology that bears his name has helped organizations in a variety of countries to achieve results and gain leadership positions in industries ranging from banking to food services, and in organizations as different as churches and governments. He is the Founder and CEO of the Adizes Institute. His work has been featured in *Inc. Magazine, Fortune, The New York Times, The London Financial Times, Investor Relations Daily, Nation's Business* and *World Digest.*

Dr. Adizes is also a noted lecturer and author. He lectures in four languages and has spoken in over 40 countries. He was tenured faculty at UCLA Anderson School of Management for 30 years and was a visiting Faculty at Stanford University, Columbia University and both Hebrew and Tel Aviv Universities. Dr. Adizes is the author of seven books that have been translated into 22 languages. His *Corporate Lifecycles: How Organizations Grow and Die and What to Do About It* (1988) is a well-regarded classic in management theory that was selected as one of the 10 Best Business Books by *Library Journal.* A revised edition was published under the title *Managing Corporate Lifecycles* in 1999. The list of all his works is at the of this book.

ichak@adizes.com

Contents

Preface

WHY THIS BOOK?

I introduced my theory of management in one of my early books *How to Solve the Mismanagement Crisis* (first published by Dow Jones Irwin in 1979 and subsequently reprinted several times by Adizes Institute). The book was translated into 22 languages and became a bestseller in several countries. It is taught in nearly every school of social sciences in the universities of Israel, Denmark, Sweden, and Yugoslavia, among others, and is still in print in the United States 25 years after its initial publication.

As I continued to work with hundreds of companies in 48 countries, my knowledge of the subject increased and I was able to expand each chapter of the original book into a book of its own. The chapter on corporate lifecycles became: *Corporate Lifecycles: Why Organizations Grow and Die and What to Do about It* (Paramus, N.J.: Prentice Hall, 1989). A new and enlarged edition of the book was published and renamed: *Managing Corporate Lifecycles*, also published by Prentice Hall, in 1999.

The chapter on how to keep an organization in its Prime condition of vitality became *The Pursuit of Prime* (Santa Monica, Calif.: Knowledge Exchange, 1997), and the chapter on how to manage change became *Mastering Change* (Santa Monica, Calif.: Adizes Institute, 1992).

More elaborations on parts of that introductory book are being presented now in a series of books. The first is: *The Ideal Executive: Why You Cannot Be One and What to Do about It*, in which I discuss why management education is barking up the wrong tree; why no one can ever be the perfect, textbook executive that management schools are attempting to develop; and I provide a new paradigm for managing in an era of rapid change.

Since the ideal executive or manager does not and cannot exist, does that mean that all organizations will be mismanaged by default? Of course not. What is needed is a complementary team, in which each team member has a different style and the tasks given to each are correctly defined and assigned.

This book, the second in the series (though each can be read independently of the others), should help you to identify your own style, learn how to complement yourself, and improve how you manage the company overall and in the long run. It will also help you to assign tasks to your staff appropriately, according to their individual styles.

The third part of the new series is a set of four books; each of them offers prescriptions for handling one of the four basic management styles–the (P) type, (A) type, (E) type, and (I) type–whether we are talking about subordinates, peers, or supervisors. Its title is: *Leading the Leaders, How to Enrich Your Style of Management and Handle People Whose Style is Different from Yours.*

Goals of This Book

This book, then, concentrates on learning how to diagnose both management and mismanagement styles, how to become alert to each style's idiosyncrasies, and how you, as a manager, can become aware of your own biases and change yourself from being a mismanager to becoming a manager and eventually, perhaps, a leader.

I am not a psychologist. My orientation is purely managerial. I am interested in how – not why – different people decide differently, communicate differently, staff and motivate differently–and in how to help them perform better.

The Premise

My premise, which I fully developed in Book 1 of the series, *The Ideal Executive*, and reiterate in the chapter to follow, is that the ideal leader, manager, or executive does not and cannot exist. All the books and textbooks that try to teach us to be perfect managers, leaders, or executives are based on the erroneous assumption that such a goal is possible. Thus classic management theorists, including Howard Koontz, William H. Newman, and even Peter Drucker, present what the manager or executive *should* do – as if all managers have the same style and can be trained to manage the same way, ignoring the fact that different people organize, plan, and control differently. The person that these management theorists describe simply does not and cannot exist.

Real executives, managers, and leaders are also real people. They have strengths. They have weaknesses. They excel in some areas and they fail in others.

This book provides a methodology to classify styles, identify their strengths and weaknesses, and predict how each style will make decisions, staff, motivate, and communicate – or, in a word, manage.

I have found that the four basic styles of management are determined by the permutation of four roles that need to be performed if an organization is going to be healthy; i.e., effective and efficient in both the short and the long run.

These four essential roles are: (**P**)roducing the results for which the organization exists, thus making the organization effective; (**A**)dministering, for efficiency; (**E**)ntrepreneuring, for change; and (**I**)ntegrating the parts of the organization, for long-term viability – or (**PAEI**).

INPUT	THROUGHPUT	OUTPUT	
The Roles	**Make the organization**	**To be**	**In the**
(**P**)roduce results	Functional	effective	short run
(**A**)dminister	Systematized	efficient	short run
(**E**)ntrepreneur	Proactive	effective	long run
(**I**)ntegrate	Organic	efficient	long run

Think of the (**PAEI**) roles as vitamins. For the health of an organization, these four "vitamins" are necessary, and together they are sufficient for that health. If one vitamin is deficient, a disease will result. In our case, the disease is called mismanagement, and it is manifested by high turnover of staff, falling market share, lower profits, etc.

For an introduction to what these roles comprise and how they conflict with each other, see the next chapter. For more in-depth discussion, see Book 1 of this series, *The Ideal Executive*.

Any permutation of the combined performance of these roles yields a style. A good manager is one in whom all the roles meet the threshold needs of the task, even if he or she does not excel in all roles. A managerial style can be a Producer, (**Paei**); an Administrator, (**pAei**); an Entrepreneur, (**PaEi**); or an Integrator, (**paeI**), etc.

A leader is someone who excels in at least two roles, one of which is (**I**)ntegration. In this book, I have not described in detail the leadership styles because once the reader understands the roles and how they generate styles, leadership styles can be imagined without much difficulty.

When only one role is performed and none of the others meets the minimum needs of the task, a mismanagement style emerges, and these are the main focus of this book. A description of each of the basic management and mismanagement styles and how they manage will be presented here. Each has its strengths and weaknesses, which will be discussed in detail.

The important message is that no one can excel at all of the (**PAEI**) roles at the same time in every situation. No one is or ever can be a perfect, textbook manager. Every human being may excel in one or more roles, but never in all four forever and under all circumstances. Good managers, however, *must* have at least a modicum of ability in each role. If any one of these four roles is missing, a foreseeable pattern of corresponding *mis*management will occur.

To evolve from good manager to leader, however, meeting the threshold requirements of each role is not sufficient. For leadership, one must perform at least two roles, one of which is the (**I**) role. And even then, whether the combination of the two roles will produce a functional leadership style will depend on this manager's specific task or on the phase of his organization in its lifecycle.[1]

DECIPHERING THE CODE

There are innumerable permutations of the (**PAEI**) code – as many permutations as there are people on earth. It all depends on the dimensions we give to each one of the elements. If we used numerals 1 through 9 instead of letters to designate each element, and kept the sequence of the elements fixed, coding would be much more specific. For instance, a (1395) manager would be strongest in (**E**) – three times as strong in this role as in the (**P**) role; second strongest in (**I**); third in (**A**); and least skilled in (**P**).

Trying to attain that level of granularity in these codes for this book is unnecessary, however, since my focus here is on tendencies and generalities rather than specific diagnoses. In addition, the codes for any style are not permanent anyway: Normal people are a composite of styles, and in a given situation they will exhibit the style that is most appropriate to that situation.

For example, people's styles can change depending on whom they are talking to. When two people meet to make a decision, one might take a position or style to complement the other person's position or style. So it can never be accurately said that a person is this or that style. What *can* be said is that someone is *behaving* right now in this or that style. What I present as a style is a behavior that a person exhibits most of the time, in most situations. It is the style this person feels most comfortable with.

For the purposes of this book, I have chosen only three dimensions for each of the (**PAEI**) roles: Excels in the role; meets the threshold needs of the job; or is deficient in the role. An upper-case letter in the code–(**P**), (**A**), (**E**), or (**I**) – designates excellence in that particular role.

A lower-case letter – (**p**) (**a**), (**e**), or (**i**) – means the manager does not excel at that role but does meet the minimum threshold necessary to do the job. A (-) designation in the code means that the performance of this role is below the threshold necessary to be functional.

LIMITATIONS

It is important to remember that no one will ever fit these archetypes perfectly. Each is a collage of characteristics, based on my observations of many people and on my imagination. Some people will fit most of a style described in the book but *not all of it*. For purposes of working with and coaching managers and leaders, it is operationally sufficient if a person's style *approximates* a style as described in the book. To progress from archetypes to real people, you have to custom-make your own predictive style using the (**P**), (**A**), (**E**), and (**I**) roles provided.

I have focused on the mismanagerial archetypes as a way of better understanding normal managers – just as psychologists study abnormal people, in order to understand normal people. Normal people are diluted abnormals. By the same token, you can dilute the archetypes presented here to understand the people you are interacting with.

A word of warning – coding a managerial style does not mean branding people like cattle. It is not my purpose to brand people, nor should it be yours as you read this book. Be cautious when using these archetypes to avoid stereotyping people. Most people probably manifest some characteristics of each of the styles. People are multi-dimensional; thus, do not decide what someone's style is and from then on simply ignore their behavior. Be alert at all times in analyzing behavior, which can change as conditions change, even during a casual conversation.

The goal, rather, is to identify a behavior *at a point in time* and know how to deal with it. Thus, although the tests at the end of this book direct you to a questionnaire that can help you identify your own general style or that of others, it would be a mistake to use this to definitively label yourself or others. The questionnaire is provided as an aid to discovering your strengths and preferences. <u>How you behave can and will change depending on the time and place and the styles of the people you are trying to work with.</u>

This book focuses on management styles only. It does not tell you what values people have. The same style could apply to Mother Teresa or a criminal. It does not tell you the IQ or EQ of the people either.

Nor is this book a survey of the literature already available on the subject of management styles. Rather, it is a compilation of 35 of observations while working with managers in 48 countries. Thus you will not find extensive footnotes in this book. For those interested in the writing of others, I am including a list of additional readings (see Bibliography).

Organization of the Book

In Chapter 1, the introduction, I define the concept of management, discuss the myth of the perfect manager, and briefly present my functional theory of management: The four roles that must be performed to achieve effective, efficient management. Next, I explain why these four roles are often incompatible, why they inevitably lead to conflict, and what to do about it.

In Chapters 2 through 6 I describe the management style that results when one role is performed with excellence and the others adequately – the (P)roducer, (**Paei**); the (A)dministrator, (**pAei**); the (E)ntrepreneur, (**PaEi**); and the (I)ntegrator, (**paeI**). I then contrast these with the mismanagement style that results when all emphasis is placed on one role while the other three are ignored: The Lone Ranger, (**P---**); the Bureaucrat, (**-A--**), the Arsonist, (**--E-**), the SuperFollower, (**---I**), and finally the Deadwood,(**----**), who does not perform any of the four (**PAEI**) roles.

Each of these chapters is organized by categories reflecting the five basic functions of every manager – decision-making, implementing, team-building, managing staff, and managing change – as well as behavior and communication.

In Chapter 7, I present some variations of the archetypes that occur when a person excels in two roles but is deficient in the other two: for example, (**PA--**) or (**P-E-**). The purpose of this chapter is to give the reader an understanding that there are endless variations of styles, depending on the infinite combinations of strengths and weaknesses in the four managerial roles.

The book ends with two diagnostic quizzes to verify the reader's understanding of the styles, and provides links to further tests online, to verify his or other people's styles.

Style and Presentation

Finally, a note on style: In writing this book, I most often used the masculine gender, because I found it cumbersome to switch back and forth and inaccurate to assign one gender to any specific managerial style. However, my insights apply equally to female managers. When, occasionally, I use the female gender to refer to a managerial style, again I intend my comments to refer to both genders equally.

The famous philosopher Ludwig Wittgenstein once said: "A serious philosophical work could be written entirely of jokes." Jokes are funny precisely because they have a kernel of hard truth in them, and humor can aid in the understanding of difficult realities. For that reason, I have included many jokes, as well as quotations, in this book to illustrate my points.

One final point: Because my theories apply not only to business at all levels but also to statecraft, to marriage and parenting – in fact, to any relationship that must deal with change – readers may find the typology helpful in understanding their non-professional relationships.

METHODOLOGY AND SOURCE OF DATA

This book summarizes for the reader my insights based on 30 years of work in the field of organizational transformation ("consulting"). Since my work as an organizational transformationist and lecturer frequently takes me all over the globe, I have been able to compare notes and share my observations with executives around the world.

I have treated companies that range from $1 million to $15 billion in sales or $120 billion in assets, and employ from eighty to hundreds of thousands of people. They are involved in numerous technologies, including aircraft, insurance, banking, the performing arts, museums, and government agencies, in both the profit and not-for-profit sectors. I have also counseled several heads of state.

I've found that my insights on managerial styles are valid for all the countries in which I've lectured, including cultures as different from each other as those of Taiwan, Japan, Sweden, Mexico, Greece, Israel, England, and the United States. Managerial styles and behavior are independent of culture–although social culture, I have noted, tends to reinforce managerial behavior.

A REQUEST

I have learned from everyone who has cared to share their thoughts with me. If any reader wishes to communicate agreement, disagreement, experience, or anecdotes, or even jokes or cartoons that illustrate my points, I would appreciate the feedback. Please write to me at the Adizes Institute, 2815 East Valley Road, Santa Barbara, CA 93108, or better yet, send me an e-mail: Ichak@Adizes.com

Thank you.

Ichak Kalderon Adizes
Santa Barbara, CA, 2003

NOTES

1. For more details, see Adizes, Ichak: *Managing Corporate Lifecycles* (New York: Prentice Hall Press, 1999), Chapters 11-12.

Chapter 1

What Is Management?

First, let's define our terms. What, exactly, do we mean by the word "manager," and what roles does the word "management" encompass?

From textbooks we learn that managers (also called administrators, executives, and leaders) plan, decide, lead, organize, control, and motivate.

However, there are organizations in which management does not perform some of those functions. Some years ago I studied the management of artistic organizations – opera, dance, theater, etc.–and I became aware that managers cannot manage artists as, let us say, one can manage workers.[1] They cannot plan, organize, and control as the textbooks prescribe. I noted the same phenomenon in the fields of health and education:[2] (A)dministrators do not perform all the functions of management. They do not decide policy matters, for example, since physicians and educators usually have this as their prerogative.

Nor do all countries around the world practice the managerial process exactly as we define it. In fact, in some countries our form of management is prohibited by law. In Yugoslavia, for instance, during the Communist era of self-management, it was constitutionally prohibited to make decisions the way we do, *for* the organization. The manager's role was to suggest, present to, and convince the workers, who had the ultimate responsibility for deciding salaries, quotas of production, investments, etc.[3]

In other countries, management is socially discouraged. In the heyday of the Israeli kibbutzim, for instance, management was deliberately rotated every two or three years, so that nobody became what in the United States is called a professional manager: a person whose profession it is to tell other people what to do.

In certain languages, such as Swedish, French, and Serbo-Croatian, the word "manage" does not even have a literal translation. In those languages, words like "direct," "lead," or "administer" are often used instead. When they mean to say "manage" the way we use it in the United States, they usually use the English word.

In Spanish, the word *manejar*, the literal translation for "manage," means "to handle" and is used only when referring to horses or cars. When they want to say "to manage" in the American sense of the word, they use "direct" or "administer."

I remember the day a salesman came to my door to try to sell me the latest edition of the *Encyclopedia Britannica*. "What do you do, sir?" he asked. "I teach management," I replied. "Well," he said," "let's see what the encyclopedia has to say about the subject."

With increasing uneasiness on his part and bewilderment on mine, we soon discovered that there was no such term in the encyclopedia. There was management science, which involves mathematical models for decision-making. There was organizational behavior, which is the sociology of organizations. But plain simple management—what millions of people around the world do day in and day out—was totally excluded.

It made me stop and think. *What is management?*

In an English thesaurus, synonyms for "manage" include: "decide," "operate," "plan," "control," "organize," "rule," "achieve goals," "lead," "motivate," "accomplish," "dominate," "govern," even "manipulate."

What is the common denominator shared by all these synonyms? They are all a one-way process. The managing person is telling the managed person what to do. Even the word "motivating" makes an assumption: that the motivator has decided already what to do, and in motivating is trying to convince a subordinate to do it.

There was a relevant cartoon in the *New Yorker* magazine some time ago: A mother who is a psychologist is trying to convince her son to take out the trash. Wearily, the boy says, "OK, OK! I'll take out the trash, but *pleeeease*, Mom, don't try to motivate me." Even the child sees motivation as manipulation. What he has to do has already been decided. It's only a matter of how to make him do it.

Now let's look at the word "subordinate"–the one who is managed, who is supposed to carry out the manager's decisions. What does that word really mean? Listen to it: *Subordinate* – like *sub*-ordinary. Now listen to the word *supervisor* – it connotes superior vision.

So the managerial process, as it is taught and practiced, is not a value-free process. It is not only a science and an art, but also an expression of sociopolitical values.

The Functionalist View

Let us try to understand the meaning of management by understanding the function it performs: Why do we need it? What would happen if it did not exist?

The function should be value-free, without any sociopolitical or cultural biases. It should be the same whether we are managing ourselves, our family, a business, a non-profit organization, or a society. Whether we are speaking about managing, parenting, or governing, it should be one and the same process conceptually, differing only in the size and nature of the unit being managed.

I suggest that an organization is well managed when the organization is healthy – and I define "healthy" as being effective and efficient, both in the short and in the long run.

Over the years I've discovered that there are four roles that management must perform if an organization is going to be well managed and thus healthy. In fact, management can be defined by these four roles, because each one of them is necessary, and together they are sufficient for good management.

What are those roles? Let me briefly define each.[4]

The Roles of Management:
A Quick Introduction

The first role that management must perform in any organization is to (**P**)roduce result s– (**P**). Why are clients coming to your organization? Why do they need you? What is the service they want? The (P)roducer's job is to satisfy this need, and fulfilling this role well means the organization will be *effective in the short run*. Success can be measured by how many people *come back* to buy your competitive products or services.

The second role, (**A**), to (**A**)dminister, means to see to it that the organizational processes are systematized: that the company does the right things in the right sequence with the right intensity. It is the role of (**A**)dministration to pay attention to details, to make the organization *efficient in the short run*.

Next, we need a visionary who can foresee the direction the organization is going to take, someone who can naturally pro-act to constant change. This is the (**E**)ntrepreneur – the (**E**) role–who combines creativity with the willingness to take risks. If the organization performs this role well, it will have the services and or products in the future that its future clients will want and seek, making it *effective in the long run*.

Finally, management must (**I**)ntegrate, which means to build a climate and a system of values that will motivate the individuals in the organization to work together so that no one is indispensable. This produces *efficiency in the long run*.

In problem-solving, each role focuses on a different imperative:

$$\rightarrow
\boxed{
\begin{array}{l}
\text{(P): what?} \\
\text{(A): how?} \\
\text{(E): when?} \\
\text{(I): who?}
\end{array}
}$$

If all four questions are not answered before a decision is finalized, then that decision will be only "half-baked." If you (**P**)roduce results and (**A**)dminister, but lack the ability to (**E**)ntrepreneur and to (**I**)ntegrate, you'll be effective and efficient in the short run—but only in the short run. If you (**E**)ntrepreneur and (**I**)ntegrate without (**P**)roducing and (**A**)dministrating, you'll be effective and efficient in the long run, but in the short run you will suffer.

For a company to be profitable in the short and long run, it needs to perform all four roles well. Why this is true is explained in more detail in my other books.[5]

If you're not in a for-profit business – if, for example, you're a government agency – then by capably performing the four roles you will achieve, instead of profit, whatever results you're looking for: service, political survival, etc.

Even parents have to perform these roles, because a family is an organization and thus a system that requires all four roles to be performed. In the traditional family, the husband performs the (**E**) and (**P**) roles, building a career and bringing home the bacon. The wife is the (**A**) and the (**I**), transforming a house into a home and a group of adults and children into a family.

In contrast, look at what we call the modern, extended, two-career family. What do you have? Two (**P**)/(**E**)s –who need a maid to do the (**A**) housework and a family therapist to do the (**I**) work.

In any organization, in any technology, in any culture, of any size, these four roles are necessary for good management. Any time one or more of these roles is not being performed, there will be mismanagement: the organization will be either ineffective or inefficient in the short or in the long run. And the pattern of mismanagement that will appear is a predictable, repetitive pattern all over the world, regardless of culture, regardless of technology, regardless of the size of the organization.

Each combination of roles creates a style. If that style is deficient in performing one or more of the roles, it is a mismanagement style. If each role meets at least the threshold needs of the task, it is a management style. Finally, if the (**I**)ntegration role is performed well in addition to at least one other role, and none of the roles is deficient, it is a leadership style.

Thus, studying the four roles, or managerial "vitamins," and who, when, how, and whether they are being performed, can be a significant tool in treating the "disease" of mismanagement.

To continue the medical analogy: If you know that the cause of scurvy is vitamin C deficiency, and you also know how to inject vitamin C, then you can treat the disease and bring the organism back to health. In the same way, if you know which missing role creates which mismanagement style and if, through training and coaching, you know how that missing role can be improved, you have a systematized methodology for coaching mismanagers to become competent managers.

In order to simplify comparisons between managerial and mis-managerial behavior, I have chosen to profile five exaggerated mis-management archetypes.

These archetypes – the Lone Ranger, (**P---**), the Bureaucrat, (**-A--**), the Arsonist, (**--E-**), the SuperFollower, (**---I**), and the Deadwood, (**----**) – represent mismanagers who are capable of performing none or only one of the four essential roles of management.

For example, the Lone Ranger, a (**P**) type who either cannot or will not perform the other three managerial roles, looks exclusively at the *what* – "*What* needs to be done?" – and never articulates the *how*. *When* is usually *now!* And *who* is probably whoever is available right then and there.

The Bureaucrat, a manager with overwhelming (**A**) characteristics, tends to look at the *how*. Bureaucrats drive the *what* and *when* of a decision by *how* it should be done. They care less if a decision is correct than whether it is implemented properly.

Arsonists, or out-of-balance (**E**)ntrepreneurs, are only interested in the *why not*. They are willing to try anything, but they don't often follow through. They give you a general idea – a kind of cosmic view–and usually want their "decisions" implemented yesterday. But ask them *what*, specifically, should be done and they will answer you with *why* they want it done.

SuperFollowers, (**I**) types run amok, are more interested in *who* is going to do the job than in *why* it needs to be done. For them, the *what, how,* and *when* are driven by internal politics.

And finally, Deadwood are those whose capabilities, whatever they once were, have atrophied completely, leaving a code consisting entirely of blanks, signifying a person whose sole interest is in not getting fired.

In my work I have discovered that the (**PAEI**) code can be applied beyond codifying behavior or style. The (**PAEI**) roles develop in a predictable sequence in the lifecycle of any organization. Over time, some roles become more pronounced and other roles less pronounced, creating a pattern of problems that can be foreseen and prevented.[6] This is very much the way parents evaluate potential problems with their children: We expect a baby to cry a lot and wet itself, but if a 45-year-old person is doing that, we know something is wrong.

In other words, once you understand the pattern, you have a tool to identify what is normal and what is abnormal at each stage of the lifecycle. It's almost like holding a crystal ball in your hand: in light of the problems you have today, you can predict your next generation of problems.

For 30 years, I have used the (**PAEI**) tools, among other tools that are covered in my other books, in my consulting work in companies around the globe – as have my associates, who are trained and certified in this methodology. It is a tested methodology for analyzing and solving problems and predicting behavior.

THE MYTH OF THE PERFECT MANAGER

The *New York Times* once ran an article about me in which I was labeled "the corporate exorcist."[7] I go from company to company trying to purge management of its belief that it can do the impossible.

What is it they cannot do? They cannot find, or even train, the perfect manager, executive, or leader.

Try the following exercise. Call all your top management into a room. Ask each one of them to write down the company's top five problems. The rules are that, first, no names be mentioned; and second, that they not use the word "because"–no explanations for the problem are necessary.

Just ask them to note on a piece of paper, which they do not have to show anyone, the company's top five most critical, significant problems, in results or processes.

All of these problems must be *controllable* by the people in the room; it is not acceptable to define a problem as something "they" are not doing. Focus on what "you" (those in the room) are not doing. In other words, instead of saying: "The problem is that it is raining," you should write: "We do not have an umbrella," or, "We do not listen to the weather forecast."

Do not look at what they have written. Do not let them share what they have written. Simply ask them: How many of the problems on your list did the company have last year? The answer is usually: 100 percent.

How about two years ago?

Most of them, right?

How about three years ago?

Again, most of them!

Now, if this is true, then how many of these same problems are you likely to have three years from now?

Most! Right?

Why, though?

Look at your list of problems again. How many of them can *any individual* in the room *solve by himself?*

None!! Right? If they could have, they probably would have.

Now ask them: How many of these problems would disappear if I gave you a magic pill that would permit you as a team to agree on the solution?

All of them, right? If you followed the instructions correctly and only wrote down problems that are controllable by the people in the room, then it is true by definition that a solution is possible if only the people in the room agree to it.

So what is the problem?

The problem is that we usually have one executive or manager chasing ten problems, rather than ten managers chasing one problem at a time.

"The problem is *not* what you have on your list," I tell them. "What you have are manifestations. The problem is YOU!!! You do not know how to work together. *That* is the problem!!!!"

And why haven't your managers learned to work together? Because the business world has been misled by misguided principles of individualistic management, which personify the whole process of management in one individual who excels at planning and organizing and motivating and communicating and building a team and making him- or herself dispensable. In other words, a (**PAEI**) manager.

But where on earth would you find this animal? Forget it; you wouldn't! That's why I call this theoretical (**PAEI**) person "the textbook manager" – because he or she exists only in textbooks. In reality, such a manager does not and cannot exist – because what is expected cannot be achieved by one individual.

> The managerial process is too complicated
> for one person to perform.

Although all four (**PAEI**) roles are necessary, they are rarely if ever performed by a single individual for each decision that that individual has to make.

This reminds me of a joke:

A preacher, in his sermon one day, said, "There is no such thing as a perfect man. I can prove it to you. Anyone who has ever known a perfect man, please stand up."

Nobody stood up.

"Anyone who has ever known a perfect woman, please stand up," the preacher said.

One demure little woman stood up.

"Did you really know an absolutely perfect woman?" the preacher asked, amazed.

"I didn't know her personally," the old woman replied, "but I have heard a great deal about her. She was my husband's first wife."

If someone has achieved "perfection," he must be dead. We have simply forgotten all his deficiencies. You cannot be alive (changing and dealing with change) and be perfect.

"The closest to perfection a person ever comes
is when he fills out a job application form."

Stanley J. Randall

Peter Drucker has recognized the complexity of the managerial task. "The top management tasks," Drucker writes, "require at least four different kinds of human being." Drucker identifies them as "the thought man," "the action man," "the people man," and "the front man." These are, of course, analogous to the styles of the (**PAEI**) model. And Drucker also acknowledges, "Those four temperaments are almost never found in the same person."[8] But he does not go beyond saying that more than one style is necessary to manage any organization. What those styles are, how they interact, how they can work together in spite of being so different, is not treated. And that is the gap I am trying to fill in this and my other books.

Management Training: The Big Fallacy

Unfortunately, management schools continue to focus on training the perfect individual manager. They make the same assumption that drives economic theory, which attempts to predict how "a firm" will behave: If you have one set of conditions, "the firm" will raise prices; if you have another, it will reduce prices. This theory personifies the group process of making a decision into an abstract entity called "the firm." It tries to analyze *why* decisions were made but neglects to explain *how* they were made.

Management theory, and management schools, suffer from the same type of perceptual limitation. Management theory, as a profession and a "science," is a 20th-century phenomenon that has resulted in a burgeoning of management training schools that attempt to equip the newcomer with the knowledge and skills necessary for good management, and also to assist the veteran in improving his managerial performance. These efforts are documented in textbooks, which are written by taking the best traits of the best managers and personifying this collage of characteristics in an individual who doesn't exist. Books in which leaders of industry share their experiences also do not meet the need, because they tend to show you only their best practices. Where do they reveal their deficiencies, which all humans have, and how they overcame them?

Most traditional management theory assumes a prototypical manager who manages all tasks–planning, organizing, training, developing, motivating, leading, organizing, disciplining–under all conditions in all organizations in the same way. It does not differentiate among the different styles and the various circumstances under which managers plan, organize, and motivate.

How many people have you known who went to the best MBA schools in the country, the best programs, who know the textbooks by heart, and still go back and mismanage? Quite a few, right? Why? *Because no one can excel in everything.*

This is where I depart from traditional management theory, which I am quite familiar with, having taught at universities including UCLA, Stanford, Columbia, Tel Aviv, and Jerusalem: Traditional management theory talks about what managers *should* do, although in reality they *cannot* do it.

Thus, traditional management training in MBA schools is, by and large, a waste of lots of money. It is even dangerous to your managerial health. You might believe, after spending so much money on training, that you can actually be that perfect, all-capable executive. MBAs are actually dangerous in their first two years out of school: they have not developed yet any humility.

So let us start over from the beginning, but this time with the assumption that being human means being imperfect; thus, every manager is, by definition, a mismanager. And that includes the management gurus.

And what should we do about that? We must learn how to complement ourselves, to cover for our deficiencies.

That is the kind of management training I believe in.

Management training as it is practiced today trains individuals to think logically and provides them with tools to reach appropriate decisions. Such training produces staff people or consultants. What it does not produce is executives who know how to work with others.

"I think it is very dangerous to believe in genius. I think it exists very, very seldom. When it does exist, it exists in terms of a man's personal or individual output, whether it be painting or music or whatever. It certainly does not exist in a corporation. Any corporation will be extraordinarily limited if it depends upon what any individual can do, even if you assume he is an outstandingly competent individual."

RALPH ABLON

WHY PERFECTION IS UNATTAINABLE

Why is it that the perfect, all-encompassing (**PAEI**) manager does not exist? One big reason is that nothing is ever perfect in itself when it is subject to change. Nothing is perfect because nothing is static.

There is a lifecycle to everything. One does not parent a baby the same way one would parent a 40-year-old son, obviously. Treating a baby as if it were an adult would physically endanger him; babying a 40-year-old would psychologically destroy him. Our parenting styles have to change as our children change; life does not allow us to stay in one place. We change, either for the better or for the worse.

There is no perfect parent, no perfect leader, and for that matter no perfect flower. Something may be perfect for the moment or, to paraphrase Andy Warhol, maybe we all get our fifteen minutes of perfection. But conditions change, and the functional synchronization of what we do with what is needed cannot remain perfect forever.[9] It may seem contradictory to say that everyone is a good leader and no one is a good leader, but it actually makes sense in the following context: Everyone is a good leader (in some situations), and no one is a good leader (forever, under all conditions).

---

*Everybody is ignorant, only on
different subjects.*

WILL ROGERS

But there is another reason why no manager can be perfect: The managerial roles are incompatible in the short run; in other words, they cannot be performed simultaneously. For example, (**P**) and (**I**) are incompatible. Have you ever attended a course or workshop where you were taught how to be a better (**I**): How to relate better to people and be a good communicator and a sensitive human being? Then there was a crisis, and time pressure, and you had to have a meeting in which you had to (**P**)roduce results, then and there. There was no time to convince, explain, or motivate. What happened to your team orientation and ability to listen patiently?

When there is time pressure to (**P**)roduce results, it is normal to become rather dictatorial and assign a lower priority to (**I**)ntegration and teamwork. The (**P**) squeezes the (**I**) out.

Let us look more closely at other incompatibilities. We all know managers who are brilliant at conceptualizing plans and ideas but not very good at monitoring the details of implementation; or who are sensitive, empathic, and good at (**I**)ntegration, but just can't seem to make hard decisions.

The explanation is simple: The four roles are not mutually exclusive, but they *are* incompatible in the short run and thus mutually inhibitive: in other words, the ability to excel at one of the (**PAEI**) roles is likely to impede one's ability to perform another.

Any combination of the four roles is incompatible, not just (**P**)roducing and (**I**)ntegrating. (**P**)roducing and (**E**)ntrepreneuring are incompatible too. How many times have you said, "I'm working so hard, I have no time to think"? In other words, satisfying present demands is so consuming that you have no time to think about future opportunities. (**P**) actually endangers (**E**), because if you work very hard, day and night, focusing on short-run results, it is difficult if not impossible to also notice the changes that are coming your way. Your mind is like a camera. You can either focus on the close-up view, rendering the long view out of focus, or the opposite.

Conversely, (**E**) threatens (**P**): (**E**)ntrepreneuring means change, and that threatens the (**P**) role. People in (**P**)roduction often complain to the Product Development Engineering department, "If you guys don't stop changing things, we'll never get anything done!" At some point, you have to freeze the planning so you can proceed with the doing.

Now let's look at another combination: (**P**)roducing results and (**A**)dministering. They are also incompatible. When you play doubles in tennis, and a ball is coming at high speed directly to the center of the court, do you wait until you're sure where it's going to land before deciding who is responsible for hitting it back? Obviously not. You both move for the ball. That is effective, because one of you will hit the ball, but it is not very efficient. However, in the efficient scenario, no one moves until the ball has landed and the players have decided who should respond to it. But by that time it's too late for anyone to return it. That, obviously, is ineffective.

When you want to be very effective, you have difficulty being efficient. That's why start-up companies, which are constantly putting out fires and dealing with unanticipated problems, are disorganized and inefficient. They accept the fact that organization and order – (**A**) – will have to wait.

The opposite is also true: If you are very efficient, you end up less effective. That is the case with bureaucracies, in which every detail is planned and no variable is left uncontrolled. The more control you insist upon, however, the more inflexible and non-responsive the system becomes, until it can no longer adapt to the changing needs of its clients.

Think of a tennis player who trains and trains until his hand and body movements are perfect. Then he announces to his opponent: "Send the ball *here!*" – to the spot on the court from which he knows he can return the ball in perfect form. I call that being precisely wrong rather than approximately right. That is how bureaucracies work. The fact that the clients' needs have changed does not concern them. They just go through the motions as developed for maximum efficiency and control. It is efficient in the extreme, and extremely ineffective.

How are (**A**)dministration and (**E**)ntrepreneurship incompatible? As you freeze new ideas for the sake of efficiency, your ability to be proactive and effective in the long run will become limited. Policies, rules, and institutionalized behavior inhibit change. Thus (**A**) endangers (**E**). And vice versa: Too much change hinders systematization, routinization, and order.

Let's look at (**A**)dministration/(**I**)ntegration incompatibility. Which country has the fewest lawyers per capita? Japan, and that is because their (**I**)ntegration is high. In Japan there is a great deal of loyalty and interdependence in business. Corporations offer lifetime employment and a family environment. They take care of each other; they are guided more by their culture than by their legal institutions. (This is changing rapidly, as (**A**) increases and (**I**) recedes.)

Now, which country has the *most* lawyers per capita? The United States. Our court system is overloaded because we rely more and more on external intervention to solve our interdependency problems. Our (**A**) is high and growing and our (**I**) is low.

As a result of these compatibility issues, most managers excel at one or two roles, are comfortable with them and tend to rely heavily on them in their behavior. It is these dominant elements that I use to characterize their management "style." While one manager (**paEi**) may excel in foreseeing the future, another (**pAei**) may excel at organizing, a third (**paeI**) at motivating, and so on. A manager, in other words, can be predominantly a (**P**)roducer, an (**A**)dministrator, an (**E**)ntrepreneur, or an (**I**)ntegrator, or any combination of the (**PAEI**) roles, but he cannot be a (**PAEI**) all by himself.

Unfortunately, for any person, a role can be completely missing, squeezed out, threatened into extinction, or never fully developed. Furthermore, change fuels our internal conflict: the more hustle and bustle in our lives, the less the four roles are in balance.

No Blanks in the Code

If the individual (**PAEI**) manager is nonexistent, then is every manager necessarily a mismanager? Of course not. Managers should excel in one or more roles but not to the exclusion of the others. Thus, the (**P**)roducing manager should be a (**Paei**) rather than a (**P---**), the (**A**)dministrating manager should be a (**pAei**) rather than an (**-A--**), and so on. An (**-A--**) style is dysfunctional–not because it emphasizes only one role but because the other roles are totally absent.

Mismanagers lack the ability to perform certain roles. Managers must excel in one or more roles, depending on their job description, but they must also be able to meet the threshold requirements of all the other roles. Why? In addition to the possibility that they may be called upon to perform one of these roles in an emergency, they must also be able to relate to those whose style excells in performing that role. You cannot build a team of four one-track-minded people. They must relate to each other.

Still, not even the best corporate leaders excel in all four roles; as a rule, they excel in (**I**) plus one or two other roles. (Whether leadership is functional to the needs of the organization depends on their task at that point in time.)

Thus the difference between managers, mismanagers, and leaders is one of degree and circumstance. A person with no dashes in his code–that is, a person who is capable of performing all four managerial roles even if he excels in only one of them – is a potentially good and useful manager without being perfect, as long as what is expected of him conforms to his ability to get the job done and as long as he is a member of a complementary team.

What purpose should managerial education serve, then, if it is not to create a (**PAEI**) manager? First of all, whether we are talking about programs for top executives or schools that grant MBAs, such programs should accept only those who demonstrate leadership traits, the (**I**) capability plus excellence in at least one other role. Next, they should make their students aware that even if they earn all A's in their classes, they are not and never will be perfect. The programs should teach their students experientially that in order to succeed, they need others to complement them. They should teach the participants how they can benefit from other managers' style differences, instead of being threatened by them. Bottom line: Students must learn how to make the right decisions and implement them well–by working with a team of people whose styles are different from theirs and nurturing trust and respect for each other, so that the inevitable conflicts among them will be constructive rather than destructive.

THE WORKABLE SOLUTION: A COMPLEMENTARY TEAM

My point is that all four roles must be performed–but by several people. For good management, people who act and think differently need to be brought together. Instead of talking about a manager who plans, organizes, etc., we should be talking about the managerial team performing these functions. The roles of (**P**)roducer, (**A**)dministrator,

(**E**)ntrepreneur, and (**I**)ntegrator must be fulfilled by a complementary team, because no one person can perform them all.

"I have never met a person who was not my
superior in some particular."

RALPH WALDO EMERSON

I want to emphasize the word "complementary," because normally when I say to a manager, "We need a team," he replies, "Yes, you are right. I am going to hire several more people like me." That is not a team. That is cloning.

Look at your hand. What makes a hand a hand is that every finger is different and that they cooperate.

"Foster here is the left side of my brain, and
Mr. Hoagland is the right side of my brain."

In the same way, we need a complementary team – a team in which the members of the team are different from each other, not similar to each other, which means acknowledging differences in style and opinion. Each person's style should complement the others by balancing their naturally biased judgments. That is a team.

THE INEVITABILITY OF CONFLICT

How do we build managerial teams in which the people are different from each other and yet can work together? Automatically, the different styles will create conflict and miscommunication, even if each member of the team is mature and capable of handling conflict.

"I never learned from a man who agreed with me."

ROBERT A. HEINLEIN

An (**A**)-dominant style and an (**E**)-dominant style are in conflict, because (**A**) is conservative and wants control, whereas (**E**) wants change. A (**P**)-dominant style and an (**E**)-dominant style are also in conflict, because (**P**) requires short-term feedback, whereas (**E**) looks to the long-term for feedback. (**E**) and (**I**) are in conflict, because (**E**) prefers to create change, which might cause conflict, whereas (**I**) wants harmony. Furthermore, in all four cases, there is misunderstanding, because each style communicates differently, sometimes even speaking the identical words but with opposite meanings.

One example is the way different styles express agreement and disagreement. If (**E**)ntrepreneurs disagree with an idea, for instance, they will usually be very expressive about it. They're expressive even when they agree. (**A**)dministrators, on the other hand, express disagreement by being silent. That discrepancy alone can cause tremendous misunderstanding and conflict.[10]

One essential goal, then, is to recognize and accept conflict and miscommunication as an inevitable and even desirable facet of managing–as long as one learns how to make that conflict constructive and how to overcome miscommunication, a matter I start to cover here and analyze in more depth in book 3 of this series: *Leading the Leaders, How to Enrich Your Style of Management and Handle People Whose Style is Different from Yours.*

LEADERSHIP AS A THUMB

I believe it is a myth that some people are born leaders, and others are born followers. I call this kind of talk "managerial racism." I believe that potentially people have all of the qualities necessary to be good managers, although these qualities may be dormant as a result of neglect. We are all, latently at least, (**PAEI**)s and can perform each role as long as we don't have to perform them all at the same time, all the time. The environment in which we operate makes our latent capabilities either grow or disappear. Unless inhibited, people rise to meet challenges and exercise any of the four management roles appropriately as they are called for.

"The role of a competent manager is to create an environment in which the most desirable things are most likely to happen."

RALPH ABLON

The difference between good management and the next level, leadership, is that a leader must excel at (**I**)ntegration in addition to at least one other managerial role.

Many people visualize leadership as a pointing finger: "Do this, do that!"

But my view is that leadership is like a thumb. Why? The thumb is the only finger that both opposes the other elements of the hand and, by (**I**)ntegrating them, helps them work together as a hand.

A manager does not have to excel at (**I**)ntegration, or being a thumb. A leader, however, does. Without that ability to (**I**)ntegrate, there can be no leadership that makes four fingers perform like a hand.

Whether the organization needs (**PaeI**) leadership, (**pAeI**) leadership, or (**paEI**) leadership depends on where the organization is in its lifecycle.[11] The appropriate leadership style must change as the organization grows and ages, just like parenting style has to change depending on the age of the child.

"Know Thyself"

The following chapters are dedicated to parsing the four basic management and five mismanagement styles and how they tend to view themselves and others, communicate, make decisions, implement decisions, build teams, deal with subordinates, and adapt to change. In addition to helping you deal with peers, superiors, and subordinates, this study should also help you diagnose your own managerial style. (This is harder to figure out than it sounds; most of us can point out characteristics in others that seem obvious, while remaining oblivious of how we affect others.)

"Make it thy business to know thyself, which is the most difficult lesson in the world."

Miguel de Cervantes

The book ends with several quizzes, designed to test your grasp of the material, and assess your personal style. Figuring out what type of manager you are is half the battle to becoming a better one.

NOTES

1. Adizes, Ichak: *Managing the Performing Arts Organization: Founding Principles in the Management of the Arts* (Santa Monica, Calif.: The Adizes Institute, 1999).

2. Adizes, Ichak and Zukin, P. "A Management Approach to Health Planning in Developing Countries." *Health Care Management Review* 2, 1 (1977).

3. Adizes, Ichak: *Industrial Democracy, Yugoslav Style: The Effect of Decentralization on Organizational Behavior* (New York: Free Press, 1971; reprinted by MDOR Institute, 1977).

4. For a more detailed discussion of this topic, see Book I of this series: Adizes, Ichak: *The Ideal Executive: Why You Cannot Be One and What to Do About It* (Santa Barbara, Calif.: The Adizes Institute, 2004).

5. See Adizes, Ichak: *Mastering Change: The Power of Mutual Trust and Respect* (Santa Barbara, Calif.: Adizes Institute Publications, 1992); and Adizes, Ichak: *Managing Corporate Lifecycles* (Paramus, N.J.: Prentice Hall Press, 1999).

6. For more details, see: Adizes, Ichak: *Managing Corporate Lifecycles*, op cit.

7. Fowler, Elizabeth M.: "The Team Approved at the Top," *The New York Times* (Business section, Sept. 16, 1977).

8. Drucker, Peter F.: *Management: Tasks, Responsibilities, Practices* (New York: Harper & Row, 1973), p. 616.

9. See Adizes, Ichak: *Managing Corporate Lifecycles*, op. cit.

10. Another source of conflict in managerial teams is divergent interests, which can lead to a lack of cooperation. That will be the subject of another book.

11. See Adizes, Ichak: *Managing Corporate Lifecycles*, op. cit., Chapters 11-12.

Chapter 2

The Producer (Paei) vs. the Lone Ranger (P---)

A Raison D'etre

The first and most important role that management must perform in any organization is to (**P**)roduce the desired results for which the company or unit exists.

What does this mean? Every organization has its *raison d'etre*. It is not put together just to be put together. Some sociologists claim that the purpose of organizations is to survive. To me, that's not normal; that's a pathological phenomenon, like cancer. An organization must have a larger mission than survival, and that is to do something or make something.

Let's use an analogy:

Five friends get together on a Friday night and have some beers. As they are drinking, someone suggests they go on a hike to the nearby lake the next morning. The rest of the group enthusiastically agrees.

The next day, the five friends follow a mountain path that leads to the lake. It's a very narrow path so they must walk single file. They have been walking on the path for hours. They're singing, whistling, joking, and laughing.

This group can be described as an organization; in other words, it has common goals that continually change and progress: First it was to get together Friday night. Then it was to have some beers. And the latest is to hike to the lake. A social scientist or psychologist would have a field day studying this primary group: Their interactions, their style, their leadership, their communication. But there is no management in this organization – until this group of five people has a task that none of them alone can perform, like coming across a big rock that's blocking the path that none of them *individually* can lift.

To lift the rock, they need to plan and organize and control and delegate. They may decide to move the rock, or they may decide to camp out right there instead of trying to reach the lake, or they may go back home and have a barbecue.

There is no management without a task, whether it is in the immediate term, the intermediate term (in which case it is called an "objective"), the long-term (which is called a "goal"), or when it is more spiritual and continuous in nature (a "mission"). But no matter which word you use, there must always be a *telos*, which in Greek means "a purpose."

"Far and away the best prize that life has to offer is the chance to work hard at work worth doing."

THEODORE ROOSEVELT

This, to me, is the first major difference between social scientists and management practitioners or students of management processes. *We have a rock to move.* It's not enough to talk about interactions and communications: Why does this organization exist? Sometimes you wonder when you look at books on social psychology: All of this interaction, but *who is moving the rock?*

So, what is the rock of a business organization? Why does it exist? What result is it supposed to give?

Profit?

We probably all know organizations that are extremely profitable and yet are going bankrupt—not *in spite of* but *because of.* Let me tell you why. Constantly thinking about profit instead of about what the client needs is as futile as saying, "The purpose of my existence is to be happy." If every morning you get up and ask yourself, "Am I happy?" you can become quite miserable. Instead, think about what *makes* you happy.

Instead of profit, you must concentrate on this: Who needs this organization? What for? Because unless you produce that for which people come to you, and do it efficiently, you're not going to be profitable. For me, profit is a *result* of good management, not the purpose of it. If you perform all four roles skillfully, profit will occur in the short and long run. The first role, (**P**)roducing, ensures that the client's need is satisfied in such a way that he will return for more. And if you produce that satisfaction efficiently, at a cost that is lower than the price the client is willing to pay for the satisfaction of that need, you are profitable. So profit is really a measurement of added value: The need is valued at a higher rate than the cost of satisfying it.

The purpose of management is to develop and maintain a healthy organization that performs all four roles. And the manifestation of that health is called profit in the short and long run; i.e., sustainable success. So one should not manage *by* profit. One should manage *for* profit.

So what, then, is the purpose for which your organization exists? What must your organization (**P**)roduce? Client satisfaction. (Please note that I deliberately did not say *customer* satisfaction. *Customers* are the particular clients of the sales department, but every manager has clients. Clients are all those whose needs your organization exists to satisfy. If the accounting department is not providing the correct budget information to the marketing department, the accounting department will have a dissatisfied client.) Find a need that you can satisfy profitably.

Dr. Karl Menninger, the famous psychiatrist, once gave a lecture on mental health and was answering questions from the audience.

"What would you advise a person to do," asked one man, "if that person felt a nervous breakdown coming on?"

Most people expected him to reply: "Consult a psychiatrist." To their astonishment, he replied, "Lock up your house, go across the railway tracks, find someone in need and do something to help that person."

THE (P)RODUCER (Paei)

Let's describe the style of a manager who excels in (P)roducing results and also meets the threshold needs of (A)dministration, (E)ntrepreneurship, and (I)ntegration. This manager, whose code is (Paei), I call a (P)roducer.

He is a knowledgeable achiever: Committed to his discipline, technically a master of his field, industrious and productive. He sells, engineers, runs the production system, or effectively completes research assignments. He is committed to getting the job done.

A (P)roducer has a powerful need to achieve. He likes immediate gratification. As a salesman, he wants to close a deal as quickly as he can. As an engineer, he loves to hear the machines humming. As an athlete, he warms up very briefly before suggesting, "Let's play," and he usually pays close attention to the score.

"Look at a day when you are supremely satisfied at the end. It's not a day when you lounge around doing nothing; it's when you've had everything to do, and you've done it."

MARGARET THATCHER

Secondly, to be a (P)roducer of results, this manager must also know what he is doing.

The knowledge component is present in all four roles, but here let us concentrate on the know-how of the (P)roducer. One cannot be an effective (P)roducer, satisfying the clients' needs, without knowing what those needs are and how to satisfy them, for which one needs to understand the technology of his or her particular discipline. I am using the word "technology" here in its broad sense: Every discipline has a technology. In marketing, the "technology" is knowing the needs of the buyers, being able to predict the behavior of buyers and competitors, being familiar with the distribution channels, and so on. In production, it is knowing how to operate the machines, knowing the raw materials of the product, the supply chain, etc.

This seems obvious, and yet you often hear the claim that a good manager can manage anything, that he can move from one technology to another and succeed: "From shoes to bubble gum, there is no difference." One merely needs to have the know-how to plan, organize, etc.

That is dangerously oversimplified, unless we add three words: *"after some time."* During that time, you try to learn the peculiarities of the organization you are managing: What makes the organization tick? How do its markets operate? What is unique to its production system? Because there are no two "rocks" alike in the world. Any time you move from one branch to another in a bank – even the same bank! – "the rock" is going to be different: Different clientele, for instance. If you move from one department to another, "the rock" is different and the needs of those lifting it can be quite different too.

"The person who gets ahead is the one who does more than is necessary – and keeps on doing it."

BITS AND PIECES, DECEMBER 1977

So what does a good manager do before he starts doing anything else? He learns "the rock." He learns what it is that his clients come to him and his organization for. If he's managing an accounting department, what is this accounting department supposed to do? No two accounting departments are the same, even in the same industry. Organizations are like men and women – everyone is different. You cannot treat them all alike. You have to know the particularities of what you are trying to manage, so that you can (**P**)roduce the expected and desired results.

The misconception that a good manager can manage anything has been particularly disastrous for arts organizations, which often fill their boards of directors with people whose experience is exclusively in business, and who attempt to run a theater as they would run, let us say, a soap company. "All you have to do," these people claim, "is produce what the clients want, budget the production, and sell."[1] This kind of approach has commercialized and destroyed many fine arts organizations.

Without knowing the essential technology, a manager's ability to make decisions is impaired. Errors will be made in the *what, when,* and *how* of decisions. The timing of actions and the degree of effort that is put into them may be faulty.[2] The side effects of an ignorant manager's mistakes can be so devastating that he ends up with more work to do than he began with – and he again performs ineptly. So the harder he works, the further behind he gets.

Such a manager, whose knowledge is limited even if his need to achieve is in overdrive, is almost a drone, stumbling ineptly from task to task, working hard but never quite getting useful results.

But being knowledgeable is not enough. Some people are very knowledgeable and yet do not produce results. They can give you a beautiful report, their judgment is correct; but they don't have what psychologists call "achievement motivation" – the urge to get in there and do it! Don't just talk about it – *do* it! This is the desire to see the finalization of a task, like a salesman who won't stop selling until he has the final signature on the dotted line.

"Nothing in this world can take the place of persistence. Talent will not; nothing is more common than unsuccessful people with talent. Genius will not; unrewarded genius is almost a proverb. Education will not; the world is full of educated derelicts. Persistence and determination alone are omnipotent. The slogan "press on" has solved and always will solve the problems of the human race."

CALVIN COOLIDGE

A manager who is technologically competent but lacks the urge to achieve will often end up in a staff position. He will be in his office, working, reading, learning, considering. When you ask him a question, he will give an extremely thorough and accurate answer. But he's not especially interested in getting things done. He likes the analytical and intellectual part of the job – a mechanism, a technology, or a system – but he doesn't like getting his hands dirty. He does not have the capability of persistence.

The complete (**P**)roducer, therefore, must know *what* needs to be done and *how* it should be done, and have the achievement drive necessary to carry those decisions out. He is a knowledgeable achiever.

The Lone Ranger (P - - -)

If you look at a car as a (**PAEI**) system, the engine would be the (**P**), the brakes the (**A**), the steering wheel the (**E**), and the oil that keeps all the pieces working together the (**I**).

Using this analogy it's easy to see why you need all the parts working together: If you have a car with a big engine but a frozen steering wheel, you have a problem.

Modern corporations, however, are usually missing some of the parts; or, if they do have all the parts, the parts aren't working together. In the case of the (**P**)roducing role, it is not good enough to have a (**P**) in your organization who is only a (**P---**); he must be at least a (**Paei**); otherwise he will be unable to work well with other, complementary members of the team. He won't get it; he won't understand the necessity or the value of their contributions.

What happens when an organization has a manager who is an outstanding (**P**), who functions like the ideal railroad engineer? You show him the track, tell him what stations to go to, give him the train, and off he goes, full speed ahead – through walls if necessary. He is such a good doer, such a good achiever, so diligent, that naturally you promote him to a higher level of management.

That's when the problem arises: He's not an (**A**), not an (**E**), not an (**I**), and I don't know why. I am only marginally interested in the why of behavior. I am mostly interested in what that behavior is and what to do about it. The fact is that he can't (**A**)dminister: Organize, coordinate, delegate, follow up, supervise, and control. He's not an (**E**)ntrepreneur: He doesn't come up with new ideas; he's not creative; he dislikes taking risks. And he's not an (**I**)ntegrator: He is not sensitive to interpersonal relations; he doesn't worry about group dynamics or individuals' feelings. He does not relate well to people.

He does not build a team or develop the capabilities of others around him – he is too busy (**P**)roducing. When a new problem is brought to his attention, he drops whatever he is doing and plunges indiscriminately into the new task. In fact, he is always rushing from task to task, from crisis to crisis. The more running around he does, the "better" he thinks he is working.

In the 1980s, I was consulting for a weapons testing center whose goal was a restructuring of the organization to reflect the needs of the clients – in this case the U.S. Navy.

It was quite a complicated situation and there was a lot of uncertainty and difficulty in deciding among the options for restructuring. In front of me sat a certain high-ranking officer, a fighter pilot, who was not participating at all. He just sat there quietly, as if he were not involved, almost as if he were not even there. He was paying attention but only marginally, and not contributing at all to the very intense debate.

Now, it is not my usual method to pull people into the group discussion. But in this case, because his high rank made his participation crucial in reaching a final decision, I finally called on him. He looked me straight in the eye and said, "Call me when you're finished and I will tell you if I like it."

That is a typical (**P---**). He was not willing to deliberate and incubate and illuminate; he did not want to go slowly and thoughtfully through the process. He wanted to be presented with the final decision so he could either approve it or veto it. The process for arriving at a decision, the consideration of many alternatives, was not his style. He was an excellent (**P**)roducer of results; however, his complete lack of the other necessary managerial ingredients made him an incompetent manager, because he could not or would not work in a team, using a systematic method, nor would he tolerate change or even ambiguity.

I call this mismanagement type the Lone Ranger. Other languages have similar names for him: In Mexico and in Scandinavia, for example, he is called "the Lone Wolf." He exists in every country.

Native Americans have something they call the "medicine wheel," which makes animal analogies to archetypes of human personalities.[3] For instance, the description of the eagle on that wheel corresponds with an (**E**)-type personality. An (**A**) they call a buffalo.

A type (**P**) personality is like the field rat on the medicine wheel. Why? The field rat is constantly running, collecting food here and there, never stopping. It's very short-term-oriented: Constantly doing, doing, doing, doing. Its vision is very close to the ground; it sees only what's directly in front of it. It is interested in a limited range of things.

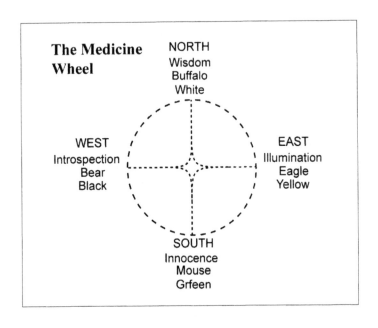

Once he identifies a task, the Lone Ranger is a good soldier. And he will get the job done. That's his advantage: He's loyal, dedicated, and a compulsive doer – but because he overdoes one aspect or role of management to the exclusion of the other roles, he can become a liability.

BEHAVIOR

What are the characteristics that typify a (**P---**) type, or Lone Ranger?

The Lone Ranger focuses on the *what*, not the *how*, not the *who*, not even the *why*. "*What* do we need to do now? Come on, guys, let's go to it. Let's not waste any more time." He does not really care if he is doing the right thing, as long as he is doing *something*. To rephrase Hemingway, he confuses motion with desired action.

Does he work hard? Yes, very hard. Too hard. When does he come to work? First one in. When does he leave work? Last one out. (The Lone Ranger would fit neither of the common inventory control labels: he isn't "first in, first out" – FIFO; or "last in, first out"– LIFO. He would have to be called FISH: "First in, still here"!)

He typically confuses quantity with quality, not realizing that quality is a totally different kind of measurement. He thinks that when he works longer and harder he is doing better, when what he really needs to do is work less but smarter.

> *Do not be desirous of having things done quickly. Do not look at small advantages. Desire to have things done quickly prevents their being done thoroughly. Looking at small advantages prevents great affairs from being accomplished.*
>
> CONFUCIUS

In fact, the Lone Ranger measures his success and his value to the organization by how hard he works. When you ask him, "How are you doing?" his typical answer might be, "I've been working till

midnight lately." And "lately," in his case, might be his entire working life!

How is his desk: clean? Never. It's piled with papers, and somehow, although he's always working hard, he's always behind, always
complaining that the day is too short. "I cannot finish. I don't have
enough time to do all the work I have to do. The new week has already
started, and I haven't even finished last week's work!"

Yet how would he feel if he came to work and found his desk clean
and nothing to do? He would panic. Why? Because he's worried when
he's not worried. He needs to be constantly doing something.

"Life is like riding a bicycle. You don't fall off
unless you stop peddling."

CLAUDE PEPPER

An executive once heard me lecture about the Lone Ranger and
told me, "You are absolutely right. I had a guy working for me who
was constantly complaining about how much he was behind and how
much work he had and that he could not work seven days a week
anymore, that his family life was falling apart. So I took it to heart
and started giving him less and less work. But instead of being happy
that finally he was finishing on time and his desk was clean, the guy
was getting depressed, very upset, and almost quit his job.

"Then I realized that he measured himself by how much he was
needed, by how many crises he had and by how hard he worked. Giving him less work did not make him happier. When he was working
too hard and had lots of crises and never saw his family, that's when
he was happiest. His complaining was really a form of bragging."

If you want a happy Lone Ranger, then constantly give him things
to do. Like kids, they need to be busy or they will get into trouble,
because if you don't give them enough to do, they might end up
charging ahead and doing something you did not want done.

This prescription applies particularly to companies in which the
founder (the "Papa") has reached the stage when he cannot lead the

organization anymore; however, he still insists on coming to work and being busy with something. In one company I coached, the founder kept himself occupied by calling clients and offering them discounts to generate sales – even though the company was desperately trying to discontinue those discounts. In a case like that, my prescription is: Keep him busy or he will end up keeping *you* busy.

Over the years, I've discovered that the Lone Ranger is an addict, just like an alcoholic. Another name for him might be the workaholic.

One of the characteristics of an alcoholic is that he's never far away from a bottle. There's always a bottle somewhere that he can put his hands on if he needs a drink. Similarly, the Lone Ranger is never far away from work. It's 11 o'clock at night; what is he carrying home with him? A briefcase full of work: In case he can't sleep, at least he can do some work.

To a workaholic, going on vacation is a punishment. It's like saying to an alcoholic, "You must go to a dry island for two weeks." That's *scary*. So what will he pack for this vacation? A trunk full of work, like an alcoholic who hides a bottle in his suitcase.

If you say to an alcoholic, "I have a bottle of the best booze there is; what should I do with it?" he's going to say, "Give it to *me*." Similarly, if you go to a Lone Ranger and say, "I have a problem; what should I do with it?" he's going to say, "Put it on my desk." In fact, the more difficult the problem is, the more likely he is to say it.

Those tons of overdue paperwork and projects on the Lone Ranger's desk aren't work. They are all bottles. Bottles, bottles, bottles.

Only when he's sure he cannot do a job by himself – only *then* will he delegate. But by then, of course, the problem is already a crisis. That is why another name for the Lone Ranger or workaholic is the manager-by-crisis. He does nothing about a problem until it has become a crisis; then he starts running around.

Like a child, the Lone Ranger has only a short-term attention span: "Let's go! What's next?" He moves quickly from one thing to another, and if it doesn't work out he loses interest and goes on to the next thing. He is straightforward and non-political to the point of being viewed as stupid. To use computer-related expression, the (P)roducer and Lone Ranger are both "WYSIWYG" ("What You See Is What You Get").

COMMUNICATION

The Lone Ranger takes things literally: "Yes" means yes, and "no" is no, even if that's not what other people really mean. Lone Rangers do not understand nuances. For them, everything is simple. Everything is literal. Give them a "yes" or a "no"; just don't give them a "maybe."

Lack of tact

In their pursuit of immediate results, Lone Rangers will plunge ahead through any barriers, often behaving quite offensively. They may say things they will later regret saying.

> *"The trouble with the man who talks too fast is that*
> *he often says something he hasn't thought of yet."*
>
> BITS AND PIECES, DECEMBER 1977

I once encountered a classic example of a Lone Ranger. He was a vice president who worked longer hours than anyone else. His subordinates were underutilized and under-trained. One day while I was working on budgetary procedure with his staff, he stuck his head in the door and asked, "What are you doing?"

"We're preparing a budgetary procedure. How about you?"

"I was making sales to pay for all of this!" he replied sarcastically.

> *Sign in a factory supervisor's office: "Caution – be*
> *sure brain is engaged before putting mouth in gear."*
>
> BITS AND PIECES, VOLUME C NO. 12

DECISION-MAKING

(**P**)s are action oriented, impatient. They do not like to do much thinking or analyzing. "Do it!" is their motto. "Shoot first, aim later."

> *"Speaking without thinking is shooting without*
> *taking aim."*
>
> SPANISH PROVERB

In the Old Testament, there is the expression *Naase ve nishma*, which means: "First let us do it; then we will hear about it (talk it over)."

Engineers are usually (**P**) types, and many are Lone Rangers. Most are trained to rely on formulas in searching for a solution to a problem. That's how they work things out: they plug in the formula and they're done with it.

Lone Rangers can't take the pain of sitting in a meeting, thinking things through. They hate to deal with uncertainty, with alternatives, with ambiguity. They see everything as either black or white; a Lone Ranger is exceedingly uncomfortable with gray. Thus they want to move fast to a conclusion. The faster they insist on moving, the longer it takes, because many problems are like a ball of string: pulling hard on one end will only cause the ball to tighten up, which means it will take longer to untangle the string.

How do you untangle a ball of string? You pull one end, then leave it alone and work on another end, and back and forth. But that's too much to ask from a (**P**). He wants it simple and he wants it now. He goes full speed ahead in the wrong direction.

This reminds me of a joke: An airplane pilot announces over the intercom, "Ladies and gentlemen, I have good news and bad news. The bad news is: We're lost. The good news is: We are making great time."

Going full speed ahead makes the (**P**) feel good – although he might be speeding directly into an abyss.

So long ago ... we were taught
That for whatever kind of puzzle you've got
You just stick the right formula in
A solution for every fool... What made me think I
could start clean slated? The hardest to learn was the
least complicated.

INDIGO GIRLS, LEAST COMPLICATED

(**P**)s often react to slow and conscious problem-solving by asking: "Why can't we just use common sense? Why are we making it so complicated?" They do not realize that we are not *making* it complicated – it is complicated. They cannot accept that it might take three days to solve a major problem.

They can be very impatient: "Just give me a solution and I'll tell you if I like it or not."– like the fighter pilot I mentioned earlier. The more they try to speed up the process, the slower it goes. They make the process more complicated by trying to make it simpler, because the more impatient you are, the less methodical you're able to be.

You start pulling at the strings uncontrollably, and the ball just keeps getting tighter. This is why, if I have a large number of engineers involved in my organizational transformation sessions, I have learned to double or triple my estimate of how long it will take to arrive at a solution that works.

On the other hand, a (**P**)'s natural tendency to simplify can be helpful in solving problems – if this tendency is controlled and he does not get carried away by impatience. Sometimes the subject under discussion *does* get too complicated and we start losing sight of the goal. In those cases, I often ask a (**P**) type what we should do, because a (**P**) can see the light at the end of the tunnel better than other people. He can be very clear; he usually hits the nail on the head. He leads us back to the highway, away from the sidetracks we got overly involved in – which is something (**E**)s tend to do.

The Lone Ranger is too impatient to read books of any length. "I like thin books," a Lone Ranger once told me. "They should tell you *what to do*, and you can decide if you like it or not, and that's it. Don't tell me more than I need to know." That's a functional orientation *par excellence*. You won't find philosophy books or spiritual books in the Lone Ranger's library. You're more likely to find how-to books of one type or another.

IMPLEMENTING

The Lone Ranger likes to be on the firing line. He prefers doing the job himself to directing others.

Let's take a (**P---**) architect as an example. He is such a good architect that eventually he heads his own firm and hires other architects and draftsmen to work for him. But when he comes to work, where do you think he drifts? Does he drift to the accounting department? No! He drifts to the design department. He watches his employees work for a little while; then he says, "OK, you're doing it wrong; move aside." And he sits down at the drafting table himself and starts drawing.

You're going to find the same problem with, let's say, the head of a hospital who is also a surgeon. He likes medicine; he doesn't necessarily like the management of it. So instead of managing the doctors, he tends to say, "Move away and let me do the job that you're supposed to do."

"I am a great believer in luck, and I find the harder I work, the more I have of it."

STEPHEN LEACOCK

This reminds me of a story about the late Kurt Herbert Adler, who was the artistic director of the San Francisco Opera for almost 30 years.

Adler had brought in a visiting director, and this visiting director was sitting in the fifth row of the opera house and speaking to the cast. "Here's what I want you to do in my opera," he said. Adler walked all the way from the other end of the hall, tapped him on the shoulder and said, "No. *My* opera."

Why does the Lone Ranger prefer to do everything himself? One reason is that he wants to make sure things are done properly. "If you want to be sure it is done right, you'd better do it yourself," is a typical expression I hear from Lone Rangers.

Also, he hates being idle; it makes him feel like a parasite. The Lone Ranger measures himself by how hard he works–so if he were to delegate, what would be left for him to do? Sit and watch others work? For the Lone Ranger, that would be unbearable. He needs to be indispensable, to have problems waiting in line for him. His desk is always loaded with paperwork and incomplete assignments. He is always rushed, and he likes it that way. Delegation would take all the fun out of his job.

"There is nothing worse than being a doer with
nothing to do."

ELIZABETH LAYTON

The Lone Ranger only delegates when it's too late or almost too late. He delegates today what should have been done two weeks ago. Why didn't he delegate two weeks ago? Because there was still a chance he could get to it. When does he delegate? When it's for sure he can't do it. That's why he is always in a crisis. His subordinates are hanging around, waiting, coming in late, doing very little. Then all at once there's a crisis: everybody's running here and there, firefighting. That's why yet another nickname for the Lone Ranger is the firefighter. He is in a waiting mode until the alarm bell is heard. It is all reactive, rather than proactive, behavior.

TEAM-BUILDING

The Lone Ranger respects other doers and achievers, other (**P**)s, but he considers (**E**)s to be untrustworthy because they constantly change their minds and are imprecise in their instructions. He believes the (**I**) type is a total waste of time, a mere politician who survives because he knows how to manipulate others. The (**A**) is also a waste of time; all *he's* good at is obstructing the (**P**) from doing his job, creating a situation in which the (**P**) has to accomplish his goals *in spite of* the (**A**).

The Lone Ranger reacts with reluctance or even downright hostility to (**A**)dministrative attempts to improve planning or communication. "We can't afford to spend too much time on the *long* run; there is too much to do *right away*," he typically responds. "If we don't (**P**)roduce results today, there might not *be* a tomorrow!" And off he dashes to make a sale or another telephone call, or to put out one of the fires that he sees springing up constantly.

Persistence

If you try to take a task away from a Lone Ranger, he can be a real bulldog: he gets his jaws locked around whatever you are trying to take away and won't let go. A Lone Ranger is so compulsive about getting the job done, no matter what, under any circumstances, that it takes a tremendous effort to dissuade him, to make him relax his jaws and move on to something else.

"Single-mindedness is all very well in cows or baboons; in an animal claiming to belong to the same species as Shakespeare it is simply disgraceful."

ALDOUS HUXLEY

And this is also how he treats others. If he is anxious and wants to make something happen, he does not touch, he hits. A (**P---**) will come down on others in an inappropriately dictatorial style, telling them what to do and when he wants them to do it – "You do it right now!" He overdoes it. He is what I call a "bicycle rider": The way he moves forward is by stepping down (on his subordinates), and the faster he wants to move forward, the harder he steps down.

Meetings

The ultimate do-it-yourselfer, the Lone Ranger hates meetings with a passion. If he is required to come to a meeting, he will come reluctantly. For these people, I have learned, sitting in a meeting and hammering out conflicts is an extremely painful process. In my lectures about the (**P**) type, I joke, "They want to (**P**) so badly, their whole body shows it." They cannot sit still. They sit there fidgeting, signing papers, writing notes, even getting on the cell phone. If a secretary enters the room with some documents in hand, the Lone Ranger calls out anxiously, "Is it for me? Is it for me?"

In a lecture, I can immediately identify the Lone Rangers, because first of all they don't come of their own free will; they are usually ordered to come. And when they do show up, where do you find them during the break? They're on the phone, inquiring: "Any problems?" Like an alcoholic who has been without a drink, God forbid, for an hour and a half, they get a little hysterical: "What do you mean, no problems?" they shout into the cell phone, as if "no problems" were a disaster instead of a pleasure.

Political Acumen

Managing, to the Lone Ranger, means managing the task, getting the job done. To him, other people are merely tools for serving that goal. He is not focused on people and their needs. As a result, the Lone Ranger is politically naive. He doesn't realize that people's judgments might be colored by their own needs and desires. He can make political blunders that lead you to seriously question his intelligence.

MANAGING STAFF

What about staff meetings? Does the Lone Ranger have them? No: "There's too much work to do, I have to run the railroad, I have no time for meetings." If you tell him he is required to have meetings, what will he do? He'll initiate a conversation, one-to-one, very likely standing in the hallway on his way to somewhere else, and he'll call that a meeting. "No time to sit. Too much work to do." He prefers voice mail or e-mail, which are quick and easy and don't require a dialogue–which he considers to be a waste of time.

Subordinates

The Lone Ranger's subordinates are the same everywhere, though their nicknames may vary in different countries. In the television series "The Lone Ranger," the subordinate was called Tonto. In the United States, they are called gofers. In Mexico, they are called *inginiero ibeme*, which means, "Go bring me something." In Israel, they are called errand boys.

Such a manager's subordinates are hardly more than spectators at a performance. Since the Lone Ranger cannot do everything himself, he uses his subordinates as "expediters," who assist him with errands and short-term assignments but have no permanent long-term re-sponsibilities. These people spend most of their time waiting to be summoned to deal with the next crisis – for which they generally have no experience or training.

These gofers and errand boys are not always low-level managers. In many companies, top vice presidents are gofers for a Lone Ranger. As a matter of fact, when an organizational chart shows an inordinate number of "assistants to the president," you can assume there is a Lone Ranger at the top.

And this phenomenon does not apply only to business executives. I have worked with prime ministers (unfortunately I cannot name them because they are still alive) whose cabinet ministers function as gofers. Cabinet meetings are a rarity; instead, the prime minister runs the country using his cabinet as a bunch of errand boys and expeditors. Trust me: I am describing something I have seen more than once.

When do these assistants come to work? Late. When do they leave? Early. What do they do in the meantime? They wait, while inside the Lone Ranger's executive office, their boss speaks rapidly and disjointedly, the phone rings constantly, and secretaries come and go in a hurry.

Does the Lone Ranger executive delegate to his subordinates? No. When you ask him, "Why don't you delegate?" he responds, "They can't do it. They're not ready. They're not prepared."

"How long have they worked for you?"

"Twenty-five years."

"So why don't you train them?"

"I have no time to train them."

"Why don't you have time to train them?"

"Because I have no one to delegate to."

Do you see what has happened? The Lone Ranger is caught in his own trap. He overworks himself, employing all of his time to (**P**)roduce results. This leaves him with no time to train others, which in turn means that he has no trained people to whom he can delegate–which means that he *has* to be overworked.

Training Others

This desire to do everything himself can be seen in the training methods the (**P---**) uses. He sees no value in the systematic *ex cathedra* classroom training of subordinates. He prefers the apprenticeship approach: subordinates learn how to perform a task by watching him do it himself. "In this business there aren't any secrets; just get the job done," the Lone Ranger insists. "If someone is willing to work hard, he should have no problem getting the job done."

Orientation

The Lone Ranger's perspective is almost exclusively local rather than global. He often gets over-involved in details, losing track of the big picture. He micro-manages; he finds it almost impossible to let go. He gets caught up in the tactical decisions, failing to recognize the more important strategic decisions. Thus, a (**P---**) is not managing, he's *being* managed. His problems are managing him.

Because everything has to go through him, he becomes a bottleneck. Since he has limited time, not everything gets done and things get lost on his desk.

This is because Lone Rangers are reactive, not proactive. They don't set priorities well. They'll attend to the squeakiest wheel rather than the most important goals. As a matter of fact, they will act only when something is broken enough that it becomes a crisis.

"I long to accomplish a great and noble task, but it is my chief duty to accomplish small tasks as if they were great and noble."

Helen Keller

You have to explain to him over and over: "You need to manage the people who perform the task, not the task itself." Ultimately, as the Lone Ranger's supervisor, you have to make the choices *for* him. You have to decide and communicate the priorities, and then you have to feed him with a teaspoon: "Now do this; when you finish, come back. Now do that; when you finish, come back."

MANAGING CHANGE

The Lone Ranger's ability to see the horizon is limited. He is typically an improviser – "All right, let's get going! Does it work? Done! *Finito!* Go! Next!" He won't take the time to pay attention to the larger questions: What is ultimately needed? What are the details that are necessary to make it work? He is reactive, not proactive. As a result, he is dismissive of long-range planning. His view of time is that it should be used to solve the immediate problems of the organization. He is not troubled by what might happen "ten years down the line."

Thus, he is always promising to plan later, "after I finish clearing my desk. Right now I have too many things to do. In the long run, there may not even *be* a company unless I get this work done." But of course he never clears his desk.

"The best preparation for tomorrow is to do today's work superbly well."

SIR WILLIAM OSLER

Since his horizon is a short one, and he is always busy with an immediate crisis; he hates changes with a passion. Change just messes things up. Because he just keeps "huffing," full speed ahead along the tracks in one direction; changing the rails might derail him.

Because he's such a bulldog, it is difficult to redirect a Lone Ranger once he's committed to a task. For corrective action, he almost needs to be hit over the head with a 2x4. In other words, only a major crisis – real or simulated – will impel him to make a change. Small impacts don't bother him; he just keeps going (often, overtime) and even if there is a major change in the situation he keeps running full speed in the wrong direction.

IMPACT OF CULTURE

The Lone Ranger is a universal phenomenon. Thousands of executives in 48 countries have attended my lectures, and invariably they could identify this style as one they are familiar with. Thus, the phenomenon is not bounded by culture, although some cultures are more (**P**)-oriented than others.

The Chinese, for example, are very strong (**P**)s. They speak less and do more. They are very pragmatic; they have "their feet on the ground." They pay attention more to what works than to intellectual arguments and theories. Religion doesn't play a big role for them. They are functional and practical; it's a very practical culture.

Americans are also a very (**P**) culture, very practical. They just want to know what works. Here's a crude hypothetical example:

In public restrooms, men apparently often throw their cigarette butts into the urinals. An (**A**) solution to that problem would be a big sign – "*It is forbidden to throw cigarette butts into the urinal!*" – with all kinds of punishments and penalties to the violators. You would expect that in a German urinal.

An (**I**) solution would be a sign that reads: "*Please leave the place as clean for the next person as you would like to find it.*" I actually saw that sign posted in the bathroom on a Scandinavian airliner.

In contrast, I once saw this very (**P**) solution in a public bathroom in the United States: There was an ashtray placed next to the urinal, and a little sign: "Please put your cigarette butts here." It was a marvelously functional solution: Since the smoker will need to get rid of the cigarette, let us provide him with an acceptable way for him to do so. There is a need. How do you satisfy it? An ashtray.

(**P**) cultures are likely to have more than their share of Lone Rangers. But regardless of where you find them, the organization that a Lone Ranger manages cannot grow, since *he* is not growing. He is inflexible and simple-minded. He can easily burn out and become obsolete. When he leaves a company, he leaves untrained people behind.

To learn how to deal with, manage, and survive being managed by a (**P---**), see my next book in this series: *Leading the Leaders, How To Enrich Your Style of Management and Handle Pople Whose Style is Different From Yours.*

SUMMARY: CHARACTERISTICS OF THE LONE RANGER

Behavior

Exclusive role: (**P**)roducer of results.
Predominant behavior: Compulsively busy.
Most distinctive personality traits: Totally dedicated to the field; hard worker.
Appraises himself by: How hard he personally works.

Communication

Focus and type of information he cherishes: Technical professional information; will share it if required to; has no time to develop it.
Typical complaints: "The day is too short"; "There is too much to do"; "I don't have enough time."

Decision-Making

Technique: Shoots from the hip: acts first, thinks and listens later.
Focus of attention: What is happening or not happening at the moment.

Implementing

How he excels: Getting things done.
If he has free time: He will find more work that he can do himself.
Attitude toward systematic management: Demeans it; claims that it takes too much time away from "running the railroad."

Team-Building

Attitude toward conflict: Annoyed with it; feels that subordinates should just get the job done.
Attitude toward other (P) types: Appreciates.
Attitude toward (A) type: Disrespects; avoids them because they tell him what not to do.

Attitude toward (E) type: Does not trust them; they change direction too often: "They are full of hot air."

Attitude toward (I) type: Disrespects or ignores them as "useless and dangerous."

Attitude toward Deadwood (----): Despises.

Managing Staff

He prefers to hire: The ever-ready errand boy: Gofers; those who can get things done regardless of direction or training; improvisers who get the job done – period; in other words, people like himself.

Subordinates are promoted: If they are always available and accept all errands supportively; if they get the job done, regardless of how or why.

What subordinates get praised for: Results.

Subordinates do not inform him about: How much they are really capable of.

Dysfunctional behavior of subordinates: Horsing around while waiting to be given something to do.

Subordinates arrive and leave: Arrive after the Lone Ranger and leave before he does.

Frequency and advance notice of staff meetings: Claims he has no time for meetings; rarely schedules them. When he must have a meeting, he calls people in impromptu and sees them one on one.

Staff meeting attendance: Dictated by the problem; usually a very small group.

Staff meeting agenda: The latest crisis; reactive to a situation that already exists or is imminent. The priority is not what is important but what is the most bothersome.

Who talks at staff meetings: Mostly top-down assignments.

Managing Change

Attitude toward change: Resists it because he has no time to institute innovations or even learn them – he's already overworked; however, will accept change only if it produces prompt, immediate results. Agrees to it when it is already obvious what needs to be done–and that usually means when there is a crisis.

Focus of creativity: Dispersed throughout the organization; allows it as long as the results it will produce are guaranteed; abhors uncertainty.

Training practices: "Do as I do."

NOTES

1. For additional discussion of the problems in role perceptions and the need for know-how in the arts, see Adizes, Ichak: "Boards of Directors in the Performing Arts: A Managerial Analysis," in *California Management Review*, 15 (1972), no. 2, 109-17.

2. For the relationship between technology and the process of decision-making, see Woodward, Joan: *Industrial Organization: Theory and Practice* (New York: Oxford University Press, 1965) and the writings of people in social-technical analysis and organizational design, such as Lou Davis and James Taylor.

3. Storm, H.: *Seven Arrows* (New York: Harper & Row, 1972).

Chapter 3

The (A)dministrator (pAei) vs. the Bureaucrat (-A- -)

When I was a lad I served a term
As office boy to an Attorney's firm.
I cleaned the windows and I swept the floor,
And I polished up the handle of the big front door.–
I polished up that handle so carefullee
That now I am the Ruler of the Queen's Navee!

SIR JOSEPH IN GILBERT AND SULLIVAN'S
"H.M.S. PINAFORE"

RUNNING THE RAILROAD

Is (**P**)roducing results sufficient? No. What happens when the manager is an excellent (**P**)roducer of results: a knowledgeable achiever? This person is so good that we reward him with a promotion. But now, he is no longer merely a (**P**)roducer. He has to work with five or six or other people, he must coordinate and delegate and control and oversee. Instead of (**P**)roducing by himself, he must make the *system* (**P**)roduce results. That is more difficult. That's why we need another role: To (A)dminister.

The (**A**) role is indispensable for good management. To (**A**)dminister means to see to it that the system does the right things at the right time in the right sequence with the right intensity, so that the organization does what it was created to do – efficiently. It is the role of (**A**)dministration to pay attention to details, to systematize the effort so that a wheel does not have to be reinvented each time a wheel is needed, and to ensure that staff follows those systems and routines. It moves the organization up the learning curve so it can capitalize on its memory and experience. It programs successes so they can be repeated.

If you (**P**)roduce results, the organization will be effective. If you also (**A**)dminister, your organization will be efficient. If you (**P**) and (**A**), the organization will be both effective and efficient in the short run.

An American analogy for management is "running the railroad." How do we run a railroad? First of all, we need the railroad engineer to (**P**)roduce results: transportation. The engineer takes the train from station A to station B. Then we need someone to manage the engineers, making sure they get the train from station A to station B, correctly and on time. The latter role, in companies, is called Operations, which is the organizational (**P**) function rather than individual.

"Ordnung muss sein." ("Order must be.")

A FAMOUS GERMAN SLOGAN

If the railroad engineer does a bad job or if Operations does not perform, then the organization is going to be mismanaged. It will not produce the results for which it exists. The trains will not run well, and the need for transportation will not be satisfied.

But running the railroad is not enough. In addition, we need supplies and money, collection and payment, and we need universally communicated timetables to get the right train to the right town at the designated time. If the schedules are well coordinated, we are running a tight railroad. That is the role of (**A**)dministration.

Some people use the terms "management" and "(**A**)dministration" synonymously. I prefer to use the term "management" for the whole process, and to restrict the term "(**A**)dministration" to the implementation and organizational parts of the managerial process.

Every manager should be an (**A**)dministrator. But is the reverse also true? Is every (**A**)dministrator a manager? No. Beyond (**A**)dministrating, a manager must also be capable of planning – deciding what work to do – which is the (**E**) role. And these roles are incompatible.

For example, a basic difference between (**A**)dministration and management is that in (**A**)dministration, especially public (**A**)dministration, whatever is not specifically permitted is prohibited. The (**A**)dministrator is given the rules by which to play the game.

For the (**E**)ntrepreneur, the conditions are reversed: Whatever is not specifically forbidden is permitted. The manager takes the initiative. He develops his own constraints within the realm of the possible and the legal.

Many managers are excellent (**A**)dministrators; they make sure that the people under them perform their tasks as planned, that standard procedures are followed. Nevertheless, they may be incompetent as managers because they do not even minimally perform the other three roles: They cannot (**P**)roduce, (**I**)ntegrate, or seek and define change – the (**E**)ntrepreneur role.[1] As a manager, such an (**A**)dministrator would actually be a particular type of mismanager whom I call the Bureaucrat.

A functional (**A**)dministration cannot and should not exist in a vacuum. It must be (**P**)-oriented: In the service of those for whom the organization is trying to (**P**)roduce. It must be flexible – (**E**)-oriented – so that it can change as its clients' needs change. And it must work well with others, the (**I**) orientation.

Notice that I used the word "orientation"; I did not say "focus." The (**A**)dministrator is focused on (**A**) but in the service of (**P**), accepting (**E**) and working with (**I**). Thus, the (**P**), (**E**), and (**I**) roles are codified in small letters: (**pAei**).

A good (**A**)dministrator is a (**pAei**); better still – a potential (**A**)dministrative leader – is a (**pAeI**). A rare (**A**)dministrator performs three roles: (**PAeI**). A (**PAEI**) leader, who can perform all four roles simultaneously, does not exist – as we have already noted.

The more roles are performed by one person, the better the management or leadership performance – as long as we do not expect this person to be perfect.

In this chapter we will deal only with two archetypes: (**pAei**) and (**- A- -**).

THE (A)DMINISTRATOR (pAei)

This person is methodical and likes his working environment to be well-thought-out and organized. When you have a business idea – especially a crazy one or one you are afraid *might* be crazy – you go to this manager to help cool your enthusiasm. He will think things through for you. He will ask you questions you had not thought of. He will see all the pitfalls you did not realize existed. Give him a business plan to read and he will tear it apart. And you will be grateful! It costs less and hurts less in the long run if problems are foreseen; either you can find ways to solve them before they become crises, or you can reject the plan as unworkable.

A good (**A**)dministrator can foresee the problems inherent in an idea. "He can find a hair in an egg while it is still in its shell," or "He can smell a rat a mile away." People have told me about such executives.

If you trust him, then if your idea passes his scrutiny, you know you can do it. And *should* do it. And if it does not pass his scrutiny and you decide to do it anyway, at least you know ahead of time what risks you are taking.

A good (**A**)dministrator always knows what is going on. He cannot sleep if he doesn't know what is going on. He keeps track of the details. He is well organized and concerned with follow-up and implementation. He has an excellent memory (or is fortified by systems, which means that he does not have to rely only on his memory), and he works to see that the system operates as it was designed to operate.

The (**pAei**) (**A**)dministrator is good at worrying, but he worries *appropriately*. He worries about precision, about integrity of information. He worries that the organization will lose its memory, its database, or its intellectual property.

A lawyer who has a (**pAei**) style is the one you want to write up your contract. But do not ask him to be your trial lawyer. He will lose in court. He can write an agreement that is faultless, but if you have to sue, find a (**paEi**) lawyer who can interpret night as day and turn a liability into an asset.

The same is true for accountants. I need two: One to advise me on my taxes – the (**paEi**) type – and the other to *file* my taxes – the (**pAei**) type. If the (**E**) *files* the taxes, I will soon be in trouble for creative accounting. If the (**A**) *plans* my taxes, I will probably pay more than necessary.

A good (**A**)dministrator is indispensable to a growing organization. A young organization usually grows too fast and in too many directions. Lacking (**A**), it can easily trip and fall on its face (i.e., go bankrupt) without even realizing that it's been going bankrupt for quite a while.

An (**E**) needs a good (**A**)dministrator more than other styles of managers: to keep him out of trouble; to pay attention to the details the (**E**) tends to ignore; to tell the (**E**) the truth; to do reality testing for him; to hold his hand when he crosses shaky bridges. An (**E**) needs a (**pAei**) to pour cold water over his head when his head becomes overheated with ideas.

A good (**A**)dministrator protects your back. He keeps the gates to the castle closed so that the enemy – chaos – cannot enter.

What he does *not* do is (**P**)roduce that for which the organization exists.

If you open a thesaurus and look for the word "administration," you will find that its synonym is "to serve." (**A**)dministration serves those who (**P**)roduce to meet the needs of the market. One (**A**)dministers *for* someone, *for* something – except in public service organizations, in which case the (**A**)dministration of those affairs *is* the (**P**) role. Nevertheless, even those public agencies need to be (**A**)dministered.[2]

THE BUREAUCRAT (- A - -)

But what happens if a manager is exclusively (**A**)-oriented? Zero (**P**), zero (**E**), zero (**I**). An (- A - -).

What is the (- **A** - -) interested in? While the Lone Ranger – the (**P** - - -)–is exclusively interested in *what*, the (- **A** - -) is only interested in *how*. That's why I call him a Bureaucrat: "Never mind *what* we do; it's *how* we do it that counts."

A Bureaucrat may be the easiest to spot of the four mismanagement types. Certainly he is one of the easiest to satirize.

Like the Navy "ruler" who describes himself in the Gilbert and Sullivan lyrics at the head of this chapter, Bureaucrats tend to rise in their organizations by following the rules, often to the point of excess. William S. Gilbert wrote the part of Sir Joseph to be portrayed with utter seriousness and sincere pride in his accomplishments. Yet his accomplishments are clearly irrelevant and insignificant.

In literature, there's a great example (also military) of a Bureaucrat. Captain Queeg, in Herman Wouk's novel *The Caine Mutiny*, has risen through the ranks of the Navy, not because he was especially competent at leading a crew or running a ship, but because he followed the rules. He says so himself:

"I don't pretend to be the cleverest or the smoothest officer … but I'll tell you this, sir, I'm one of the stubbornest. I've sweated through tougher assignments than this. I haven't won any popularity contests, but I have bitched and crabbed and hollered and bullied until I've gotten things done... *by the book*."[3] (Italics added.)

Let us reread what Captain Queeg says once again and codify it in (**PAEI**) terms:

"I don't pretend to be the *cleverest [no (E)]* or the *smoothest* officer *[no (I)]* ... but I'll tell you this, sir, I'm one of the *stubbornest [this is (P)]*. I've sweated through tougher assignments than this *[more (P)]*. I haven't won any popularity contests *[no (I)]*, but I have bitched and crabbed and hollered and bullied *[more (P)]* here until I've gotten things done ... *by the book [(A), big-time]*".

"Now, I'm a book man *[more (A)]*, as anyone who knows me will tell you," Queeg tells his sailors proudly. "I believe the book is there for a purpose, and everything in it has been put in it for a purpose. When in doubt, remember we do things on this ship by the book *[more (A)]*. You go by the book and you'll get no argument from me [(A) again].You deviate from the book and you better have a half dozen damn good reasons–and you'll still get a hell of an argument from me *[even more, bigger (AAAA)]*. And I don't lose arguments on board this ship."[4]

A particularly extreme example of bureaucratic compulsiveness occurs in the novel during a typhoon, when it appears that Captain Queeg is prepared to let his ship sink rather than disobey an order.[5]

While the (A)dministrative role is a necessary component of the managerial process, a disproportionate emphasis on (A)dministration can be counterproductive. The more centralized a system is, the more (A)dministrative, rather than managerial, is the job of middle management. It is the (- A - -)'s bureaucratic tendencies that impart much of the hierarchical nature to organizations.

BEHAVIOR

What are the characteristics that typify an (- A- -) type, or Bureaucrat?

The Bureaucrat spends an *excessive* amount of time worrying about (A)dministrative details. He prefers to do things right rather than do the right things. In other words, he would rather be precisely wrong than approximately right.

Here's a story that will illustrate this point: I was flying over Brazil some years ago. Sitting next to me was a leading accountant from a leading accounting firm, a big (- **A**- -). We were looking through the window, and we saw the Amazon River. He said, "Dr. Adizes, do you know how old this river is?"

"No," I said.

"It is a billion years and seven months old."

"How did you get a billion years and seven months old?" I asked, amazed.

"Well, seven months ago someone told me it was a billion years old."

That is what I call precisely wrong. In business, something similar can happen. A Bureaucrat can give you a budget of a million, three hundred thousand dollars and fifty-five cents … in the wrong direction. The numbers are precise, but the reason for spending the money may not be clear at all.

"The chief danger in life
is that you may take too many precautions."

ALFRED ADLER

Here's another example: If you ask a Bureaucrat to give you a report analyzing whether your company should try to penetrate the New York market, he'll say, "Sure," and disappear for a while. He'll accumulate data and analyze it ad infinitum. He'll work hard to make the uncertainties disappear. But by the time he comes back with his recommendation, that market may already have been claimed by your competitor. Why? Because the Bureaucrat prefers not to take risks. He does not want to be embarrassed by making the wrong decision. He wants everything safe and precise. He's precisely wrong.

Here's a joke that makes that point:

Two men were flying in a hot air balloon and became lost in the fog. After a while they descended from the fog and tried to find out where they were. They spotted a man on the ground, walking along a path, and shouted to him, "Where are we?"

The man on the path answered, "You are in a balloon!"

The two men gave the balloon some hot air and ascended again into the clouds. One man turned to the other and said, "You know, that guy on the path was an accountant."

"How do you know that?"

"Because what he said was precisely right … and totally useless!" the first man responded.

"The motion has been made and seconded that we obey the law."

Bureaucrats pay attention to the form, to the number to the very last digit—at the expense of the total picture. The Bureaucrat may be focused on the wrong market, the wrong product – the wrong direction! – but his reports always look very good because the numbers are calculated to the third decimal.

"Statistics are no substitute for judgment."

HENRY CLAY

When does he come to work? On time. When does he leave work? On time. How is his desk? Clean, all in neat piles.

He wants everything to be perfect and under control, and he is capable of spending an inordinate amount of time and money on a marginal control that is really not worth it. Such demanding perfectionism can suffocate a company.

The Bureaucrat behaves as if he believes that form produces function. Now, sometimes that is true; that is why everyone in the military has to polish his shoes, shave, and have his hair cut the same way; that's why there is all that exacting discipline and marching in formation, where you cannot move your head one inch to the left or one inch to the right. Military leaders assume that the form produces the function, that if you polish your shoes and shave exactly as required and hold your head exactly as required and march exactly as required, when the time comes and they tell you to go and attack and sacrifice your life, you will run and do exactly as instructed. So the form will produce the function.

But here is the danger: Sometimes the form is so inflexible that it will not produce the function. That's why partisans and guerrilla forces invariably defeat organized establishment armies: they rely more on (**I**) than on (**A**) in asking people to put their lives on the line.

We can see this confusion of form and function with Captain Queeg in *The Caine Mutiny*. There is a war on, but what is he obsessing about? Who stole the strawberries from the ship's refrigerator – as if appointing a committee to investigate the alleged theft will bring about the desired discipline and dedication to win the war.

The Bureaucrat has an organizational chart readily accessible – if it is not on paper it is in his head. He has no trouble finding any of the organization's rules or procedures at a moment's notice, and if they do not exist he will make them up on the spot: "From now on this is the new policy…," he might say. He manages by means of directives, usually in writing. Even when violations are necessary to produce the right results, he won't tolerate his subordinates' breaking the rules. He sees the mission of the system as a direct product of the form and thus makes the system's implementation and its protection a primary goal.

Free Time

We've seen that the (**P**) abhors free time. If he has nothing to do he will find some new task to perform. The Bureaucrat's free time, on the other hand, is spent looking for new transgressions against the system. When he finds one, he designs a new form, a new report, or a new policy that will prevent the transgression from being repeated.

Doubts

Like the Lone Ranger, the Bureaucrat is very literal-minded. An (-**A** - -) needs to see something for himself in order to believe it. He needs to be sure.

He also needs to be sure there is no risk before he will act. But because he is reluctant to take risks, he rarely learns anything new.

To say something like, "I'm not sure, but it appears to me ..." is typical for an (**E**), but an (- **A** - -) has difficulty saying it. An (**E**), for example, looking through the fog and seeing a big ear and a big leg and a big back, might say: "Aha, that must be an elephant." He fills the information gaps with his imagination to see the pattern and come up with a conclusion. But an (- **A** - -) will not infer anything. The big ear and the big leg and the big back do not add up to an elephant, until the fog rises. Then he'll go and touch the elephant and smell the elephant, and then – hesitantly – he might say, "Aha! *Maybe* it's an elephant."

The (**A**) way of reasoning is that until proved beyond doubt, nothing should be assumed.

COMMUNICATION

Here is a story about how obsessive concern with the written word instead of with common sense can lead to absurd results. This story, which I read on the Internet, was the first-place winner in a recent Criminal Lawyers Award contest in the United States. Even if it is not accurate, it is interesting in that it shows how the (**A**) role is out of control in our society:

A Charlotte, N.C., lawyer purchased a box of very rare and expensive cigars, then insured them against fire, among other things. A month later, having smoked his entire stockpile of these great cigars and without having made even his first premium payment on the policy, the lawyer filed a claim against the insurance company. In his claim, the lawyer stated the cigars were lost "in a series of small fires."

The insurance company refused to pay, citing the obvious reason: that the man had consumed the cigars in the normal fashion.

The lawyer sued and won! In delivering the ruling, the judge agreed with the insurance company that the claim was frivolous. The judge stated, nevertheless, that the lawyer held a policy from the company in which it had warranted that the cigars were insurable and also guaranteed that it would insure them against fire–without defining what it considered to be "unacceptable fire"– and thus was obligated to pay the claim.

Rather than endure a lengthy and costly appeal process, the insurance company accepted the ruling and paid $15,000 to the lawyer for his loss of the rare cigars, lost in the "fires."

But after the lawyer cashed the check, the insurance company had him arrested on 24 counts of ARSON!!!!

With his own insurance claim and testimony from the previous case being used against him, the lawyer was convicted of intentionally burning his insured property and was sentenced to 24 months in jail and a $24,000 fine.

This incident, true or not, is a good example of how the written word dominates at the expense of common sense.

"People have rules for when they can't trust their instincts."

KENNETH A. FISHER

Manualitis

(- **A** - -)s are prone to a managerial disease called "manualitis": If it can be codified into manuals, then it *should* be. Everything is documented, processes are written, and the written word begins to dominate the organization's behavior. One characteristic of bureaucratic organizations is its worship of the written word.

Whenever Bureaucrats find deviations from the system, they correct them by creating more rules and manuals. So what's going to happen? The new manuals will create even more opportunities to find deviations, because the granularity of what is being controlled is increasing. So there are going to be even more controls, which call for even more manuals and more policies and more rules, which are grounds for even more deviations, thus for even more controls and rules, all becoming progressively more minute – to the point where they actually can paralyze the company. No one is serving the clients anymore. They are all busy reading and writing reports, controlling each other.

"I'm sorry, dear, but you knew I was a bureucrat when you married me."

The Bureaucrat behaves as if he believes that everything should be organized for maximum efficiency. But efficiency can be detrimental to effectiveness, because when behavior is too extremely codified, a manager might not be free to react quickly enough.

There's a story I like about Jan Carlzon, the president of SAS in the 1980s. The first day he came to work after being appointed to the top managerial role, he called his management team together, put all the company manuals on a table and with one big swoop he flung them onto the floor and said, "Let's start from the beginning."

Why? Because he knew that bureaucratic controls reproduce themselves: There is always another way to break down and codify an action. Another problem is that, once everything is codified, usually with acronyms, you have to know this special language in order to understand what's going on.

People who are managed by an (- **A** - -) spend an enormous amount of time reading memos and writing memos and filing memos and responding to memos. This cuts down efficiency tremendously. It may look like the system is very efficient because it's all laid out in black and white, but what's really happening is that everyone is wasting time documenting every single action.

Decision-Making

When you ask a Bureaucrat to diagnose a problem, he usually starts all the way back with Adam and Eve, and then takes you through the entire history of the problem – first what happened and *then* what happened and *then* what happened and *then* what happened. It's endless. He believes this is necessary, that he must tell you the entire history of the problem in order for you to understand it.

Given his 2,000-year perspective on the problem, a Bureaucrat naturally thinks it's going to take another 2,000 years to solve it. In the field of management this is called "paralysis from over-analysis." A Bureaucrat is capable of analyzing forever, creating a process that's very complicated and difficult, in which actual results cannot happen. It's just too complicated.

"The man who says it cannot be done
should not interrupt the man doing it."

CHINESE PROVERB

He sees the problem in the past and the solution in the future. You might say this is logical – except that it is not how the other styles approach problem-solving. The (**P**) is focused neither on the past nor on the future. He is focused on the here and now: "What needs to be done now, let us do it."

The (**E**), as we will see in the next chapter, sees the problem in the future –"There are so many opportunities that need to be taken care of"– and, oddly enough, he expects the solution to have been handled already in the past and is usually impatient: "How come we haven't done anything about this already?"

The (**E**) actually detests the (**A**), whom he considers to be an obstructionist, not too intelligent, slow, and not a true partner in building a company: "He lives on a different planet"– which is exactly what an (**A**) says about an (**E**) and what a (**P**) says about both of them.

A Bureaucrat is also very cost-conscious – too much so. He knows the cost of everything but the value of nothing, for the following reason: The cost is for sure, the value is maybe. So he discounts the value, which is a maybe, and focuses only on the cost, which is for sure.

He will tell you, "We cannot do this, it's too expensive." But the truth is that very often the cost of *not* doing may be higher than the cost of doing. I'll give you an American expression that exemplifies this principle: "If you think education is expensive, think of the alternative."

"Obstacles are the things a person sees
when he takes his eyes off his goal."

E. JOSEPH COSSMAN

This characteristic of focusing on the cost and discounting the value of the expense makes marketing people apoplectic: "Unless we penetrate the market we're going to have nothing. We're feeding the dog with his own tail! We are not moving anywhere; we are just in a holding pattern. We *must* be moving into new markets." But an (- **A** - -) will prefer not to take the risk or spend the money. He will spend time asking for more information and more details and more justifications and more studies and more analyses–all to minimize risk. But time costs money, and meanwhile the opportunity will slip away.

To use a tennis analogy: An (- **A** - -) probably prefers to wait until he knows exactly where the ball is going to land before he goes to hit it. But by that time, of course, it's too late. Afterwards, he will come up with all kinds of explanations: "The ball was going too fast"; "I couldn't see it fast enough"; whatever. But what's the difference? The fact is, he didn't hit the ball.

An (**E**)-style manager, on the other hand, will proact. He will try to imagine where the ball is going to land and go there and get ready to hit it. Now, sometimes he will guess wrong and miss the ball because it landed somewhere else. Nevertheless, it's better to be approximately right than precisely wrong.

If the game is a very slow one, the (- **A** - -) might hit the ball even if he waits to see where it will land. So, in a slow-moving market or economy, waiting and knowing for sure may not be a bad decision. But in a fast game, where the balls fly at a tremendous speed – and because of globalization and the Internet and tremendous technological advances, that is what the modern world looks like – you must move at least at the speed that your world is changing, and for that you must be proactive.

Being an (- **A** - -)-type decision-maker in a fast-changing market is a prescription for failure.

IMPLEMENTATION

Exclusive Focus

The Bureaucrat can subvert the goals of the organization through his insistence on observing the letter of the law, even when departures from it are essential. His primary and often exclusive commitment is to the implementation of a plan, regardless of its wisdom or even its ethics.

At his 1961 trial in Jerusalem for implementing the genocide of European Jewry, Adolf Eichmann's defense was a morbid and extreme example of this type of behavior. Eichmann described his role in the Third Reich as having been "an administrator of trains." The fact that at one end of the railway line were the homes of the victims, and at the other end were the extermination camps, did not preoccupy him. Eichmann maintained that the ultimate goal of his operation was irrelevant, and that his responsibility was confined to ensuring the efficiency of train operations.

Changing a Decision

Bureaucrats frequently have difficulty revisiting a decision during the implementation phase. This is often necessary, because while you are implementing the decision you made, the conditions you based that decision on may have changed. The world often changes even faster than you can implement a plan to adapt to the changes.

"Nothing endures but change."

HERACLITUS

A typical Bureaucrat resists such change. "We decided," he'll say. "We spent a lot of time on this decision! We spent a lot of money on it! We spent a lot of effort on it! We are not going to open this chapter again!"

Cost of Implementation

While the Lone Ranger evaluates himself by how hard he works and by the results he achieves, the Bureaucrat evaluates himself by how well he *controls* the system and by his success in eliminating deviations and minimizing uncertainty. Because of this, he tends to be a crowning example of Parkinson's law.[6] He gets increasing numbers of subordinates to implement the same task, trying to control every detail, without achieving any apparent increase in productivity.

Over time, the department managed by the Bureaucrat will perform the same duties, but utilizing more and more people who must follow increasingly complex procedures to assure maximum conformity and minimum uncertainty. The end result is the opposite of what the (- **A** - -) intended. The role calls for efficiency, but the result of this mushrooming bureaucracy with no apparent increase in productivity is just the opposite: an extreme *in*efficiency.

TEAM-BUILDING

Handling Conflict

The Bureaucrat abhors interpersonal conflict. He feels that such conflict will "rock the boat" and endanger his control of the system. Therefore, he prohibits it. As a result of his insistence that it should not exist, people sweep it under the rug.

In a bureaucratic organization, everything looks very organized, clean, and perfect; just don't lift the rug! What you would find under there are problems that have been buried beneath the rug for a long time, and dangerous conflicts that could destroy the company, left to fester.

"Administration means a rejection of the idea of conflict as a desirable element of society. Administration wants extremes adjusted; it wants differences settled; it wants to find which way is best and use that way exclusively."

CHARLES REICH

Why are there so many conflicts and why are they so deep? Because the company has not addressed them. Things either get better or worse in life, and if they do not get addressed and made better, they will have to get worse, because nothing stays in one place. Life is change, and change – for better or worse – is life. Since the Bureaucrat rejects change and refuses to address the conflict that necessarily accompanies change, that conflict is continually growing and expanding, like mold or cancer.

Or there might be a different outcome: No conflict. Truly. Some of the happiest organizations I have ever seen are bureaucracies. There is no conflict. Everyone gets along very well with everyone else. They come on time, leave on time, and there is no conflict.

What is going on here? Nothing. It is dead. That is why there are no conflicts. The organization is totally ineffective. It goes through the motions: processes paper, does exactly what the procedures prescribe. But nothing is being accomplished. So why would there be conflict? About what?

Take the United States Immigration and Naturalization Service (INS), for instance. Weeks after terrorists struck the World Trade Center, killing themselves and 3,000 other people, the INS approved student visas for some of those terrorists. The INS processed the paperwork. Everything was done by the book. But the goal–of protecting the country from hostile elements – was missed.

Process of Reasoning

Bureaucrats are linear thinkers: A, B, C, D, E, F, G. They do not understand that sometimes C relates to H and H relates to A and A relates to J and J relates to B. They get very upset when they perceive a discussion as getting out of order. It's too complicated for them: "Stop! What are you talking about? Where are you going and why are we discussing this? Why is it relevant?"

This reaction is also characteristic of a (**P - - -**). Both insist that discussions proceed in a linear progression. This kind of request will drive an (**E**)ntrepreneur absolutely crazy; to him, everything is related to everything else. An (**E**) thinks in a non-linear flow of consciousness that confuses the daylights out of an (**A**) and frustrates the hell out of a (**P**).

Discussions do need to be open to lots of different options, but an (- **A** - -) can't see that. You have to tell him, "Relax, we're just exploring different alternatives, and of these different alternatives there could be different interpretations of how they are going to advance and change."

Handling of Information

The Bureaucrat wants total control of all information of an (**A**)dministrative nature – information that involves "how to get things done right." Proposing a budget may entail a hundred steps. Hiring or firing someone may require filling out dozens of forms, and so on.

---

*"Don't be afraid to take a big step if one is
indicated.
You can't cross a chasm in two small jumps."*

David Lloyd George

When I reorganize a company, I assign a color to each department. These colors designate accountability. For example, the department labeled green is the one responsible for profits. The red one is overhead. The brown one charges for its services or products at cost.

Once that's done, you can look at an organizational chart and see immediately who is responsible to whom for what. Often some surprises come out of those discussions. Who should be green? Which department is really the profit center? Sometimes it's the product group, but the profit center can also be based on geography; it could be the market; it could be a phase in product development. It could go lots of ways.

Bureaucrats usually get very upset during this process: "You're going to mess up our database, you're going to mess up information! We are going to lose control!" They want to know what the heck you're doing and exactly how much it's going to cost and exactly what benefits will result. They don't see that the main benefit lies in clarifying and sorting out who is responsible for what, and that its value cannot be measured in dollar terms.

As President Eisenhower once said, "Plans are useless. Planning is priceless." It is the thought process that gets you all the benefits. If you understand the *whats, whys, whos,* and *hows* and have run all the scenarios, it will be easy to change the plan when the situation changes – and it will change.

MANAGING STAFF

Hiring

The Bureaucrat hires people like himself – people who do as they are told and will not take the initiative. They do not ask questions that challenge the status quo; they do not rock the boat. Subordinates come on time and leave on time; what they do in between is not as important. That's one way in which the Bureaucrat assumes that the form will produce the function.

I call the Bureaucrat's subordinates yes-yes men or office clerks. But please note: Although they have a clerk mentality, they are not necessarily clerks. They could be vice presidents earning $100,000 a year or more. Regardless, they have to come on time, leave on time, and do everything by the book.

Office clerks always agree with the Bureaucrat, always comply and do exactly what he wants, and never lift a hand beyond that.

There's even a joke about this kind of subordinate: A new person arrives in Hell and is sent to a bureaucratic department in Hell to work. When he gets there he finds that all the other workers are standing in fecal matter up to their lips. Horrified, he asks, "How do you work here?"

"Just don't make waves!" is the reply.

The only important thing is not to make waves. Just like Sir Joseph in *The H.M.S. Pinafore*, as long as you come on time, leave on time, and make no waves, you might even be promoted to president. That's a typical Bureaucrat.

The Lone Ranger will accept a subordinate's violations of procedure as long as good results are achieved. The Bureaucrat, however, is exclusively concerned with the methods used to achieve the results. Let us take the example of a salesman who has produced some extraordinary, unexpected, unplanned-for sale. If the salesman works for a Lone Ranger and tries to tell him how he accomplished it, the Lone Ranger will say, "Great, great, but tell me about it later," because the Lone Ranger is busy with his own efforts.

A Bureaucrat, on the other hand, will want full details of exactly what the salesman did. But the moment he finds out what it was that the salesman did differently, he will stop the inquiry and focus on how that difference is actually a transgression or violation of the rules.

From that point on, the Bureaucrat will forget the results that were achieved and focus solely on the transgression: How dare the salesman violate a rule or procedure? He's playing a game that Eric Berne wrote about in his book *Games People Play*, called: "I Got You, You S.O.B."[7]

So naturally, salesmen who work for a Bureaucrat learn never to make waves, and as long as they are paid well, they suffer the pool of fecal matter, keep working by the book, and keep their mouths shut. If that creates no results, "Well, that's life," they shrug.

Staff Meetings

Does the Bureaucrat hold staff meetings? You bet your life: every Monday and Friday from 9 to 12. Secretaries take minutes; the last meeting's conclusions are discussed and verified as to their implementation. There is order, and along with it there is boredom with the myriad details that the Bureaucrat insists on covering.

Does he have an agenda? Absolutely. In detail. Does the agenda deal with important subjects? Not necessarily. Assignments are discussed, but instead of emphasizing their purpose and validity, the discussion centers on *how* they will be implemented. The company might be losing market share, even going bankrupt, but the Bureaucrat will be droning on about the need to fill out the necessary forms in duplicate and on time. That's why I say he runs a very well-controlled disaster: The company's going broke, but on time!

The Bureaucrat's subordinates learn never to show deviations, never to show turbulence, never to acknowledge problems. Conflicts and problems are swept under the rug.

Why? Because the subordinates know that if they reveal these problems, there are going to be meetings; there are going to be investigations; the Bureaucrat is going to have to find out who did it, why, how, where, and when. There are going to be consequences – more rules, more manuals, more control. In a word, there is going to be a witch-hunt, which will make things even tougher for the staff.

So to avoid that situation, the Bureaucrat's subordinates assure him, "Everything is under control," when in reality it ain't so. The Bureaucrat hears silence and assumes the silence signifies order and efficiency. But often, just the opposite is true.

As long as there is noise, you know what is happening. When there is silence, you don't know anything. It can mean total apathy: people have given up and don't want to work anymore. Or it might be the calm just before a total eruption of rejection and revolution.

Are you a parent of small children? If they are in their room playing, when do you get concerned: When they are fighting and there is noise, or when there is absolute prolonged silence?

Training

The Bureaucrat loves training. He wishes he could program everybody and make every process a routine.

Permission to Change

What is an (- **A** - -)'s typical answer when a subordinate asks for permission to do something different? "No." Before you even finish the sentence: "No." Here is a typical Bureaucrat on the phone (this is a Russian joke): "No. No. No. Yes. No. No. No."

"What was that one 'yes' about?" you ask him.

"He asked me if I heard him clearly."

MANAGING CHANGE

Change, to a Bureaucrat, is a threat of major proportions, and the Bureaucrat will keep on hand a never-ending arsenal of reasons for fighting it. His ingenuity in finding reasons to discourage new projects makes him an obstructionist. The organization has to achieve its goals in spite of him, and those individuals in the organization who are committed to getting things done learn to bypass him in trying to implement change.

Strategic planning usually entails analysis of threats and opportunities. But the Bureaucrat hardly ever sees opportunities, and he regards change as a threat. Under the Bureaucrat, strategic planning is at best an exercise in forecasting, and quite often it simply analyzes the past and projects it into the future.

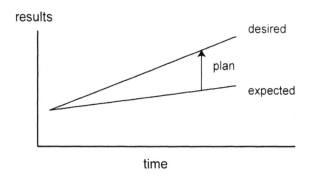

So what is next year's budget or goal? "What we are sure we can achieve. How about some sure number above the one we reached last year?" is the Bureaucrat's typical approach. A Lone Ranger, in contrast, will have no plans for next year. He is too busy working to take the time to plan for next year. "Who can predict next year anyway? It's a waste of time to try," is a typical Lone Ranger attitude toward planning. An (E), on the other hand, simply plans to implement what he desires, and the hell with what's expected. (See the chart above.)

A consultant once told me that when he worked for an accountant, a change in budget was the equivalent of giving birth. It took months to accomplish, and "delivery" was accompanied by great labor pains.

---

*"It is horrible to think that the world could one
day be filled with nothing but those little cogs,
little men clinging to little jobs and striving
toward bigger ones—a state of affairs which is to
be seen once more, as in the Egyptian records,
playing an ever increasing part in the spirit of
our present administrative system, and especially
of its offspring, the students. This passion for
bureaucracy is enough to drive one to despair."*

Max Weber

One reason for this is that the Bureaucrat abhors ambiguity. He cannot comprehend that inaction in times of change is much worse than ambiguity. Unlike an (E)ntrepreneur, a Bureaucrat does not sense a trend, cannot interpret clues in the fog. He always prefers to wait for certainty, even if waiting means losing the opportunity. That's why a Bureaucrat never starts a company; only (E)s start companies. Bureaucrats want a plan, but they hate the planning. Once the plan is produced, even if the planning process isn't explicitly understood, that plan is set in concrete. Try changing it. You will encounter enormous resistance.

In my methodology, I request that every plan include the assumptions on which it is built, either up front or in an appendix. Management must continually monitor those assumptions. It is important to manage by assumptions; when the assumptions are not relevant anymore, you can assume that the plan isn't going to work either.

George Soros, one of the richest self-made men on earth, says in his book *Soros on Soros: Staying Ahead of the Curve* [8] that the secret of his success is not that he is smarter than the other people in the arbitrage industry. He just identifies his mistakes sooner and corrects them sooner. That is an (**E**) for you. Not an (**A**), for sure.

Nothing is stagnant. In other words, don't get overly attached to that plan you've produced, because as the situation changes you will have to change the plan. Watch and monitor your assumptions as closely as you can; articulate them as well as you can.

For example, the color we give to a department in my accountability exercise may change tomorrow, because conditions might change. Today we are going to run the profits by product and not by market. But if there's suddenly a lot of competition, the market's orientation rather than the product orientation may begin to drive the decision-making.

What is important is to stay flexible enough to deal with such changes. As the factors change, you may need to change the decision. (- **A** - -)s have trouble with this, because there are too many factors and in modern markets most of them are not controllable.

CONCLUSION

By the time the Bureaucrat is eliminated from an organization, that organization may have become so mired in regulations and rules that it will have difficulty adapting to long overdue changes, either internally or externally or both. Innovations in a bureaucratic system are not made easily, and "surgery" is often needed. People are fired, and new blood is called in. This is a trauma from which organizations need a long time to recover.

In addition, a new manager may have a great deal of trouble trying to alter the established procedures, and may ultimately find it impossible. Sometimes the new manager winds up adapting himself to the faulty system because he cannot change it.

Summary: Characteristics of the Bureaucrat

Behavior

Exclusive role: Implementer, (**A**)dministrator.
He arrives at and leaves work: On the dot.
How he excels: Putting and keeping things in order.
Most distinctive personality traits: Meticulously organized, slow and careful, thoughtful, conservative.
Appraises himself by: How placid and how well controlled the office is.
Typical complaint: Someone violated some rule or procedure.
If he has free time: He will think of new forms, controls, etc.

Communication

Focus and type of information he cherishes: (**A**)dministrative.

Decision-Making

Technique: Follows existing decisions; sees opportunities as threats.

Implementation

Predominant behavior: Controlling implementation.
Focus of attention: How work is being done.

Team-Building

Attitude toward conflict: Ignores it or fights it, depending on whether or not it threatens his ability to control.

*Attitude toward (**P**) type:* Qualified criticism: "He is just running around."

*Attitude toward other (**A**) types:* Approves.

*Attitude toward (**E**) type:* Abhors: "Full of hot air!"

*Attitude toward (**I**) type:* Suspicious.

Attitude toward Deadwood (- - - -): Likes them.

Managing Staff

Subordinates' style: The Bureaucrat hires yes-yes men, otherwise known as office clerks.

Subordinates arrive and leave: On the dot.

Frequency and advance notice of staff meetings: Frequent, regular, and scheduled.

Staff meeting attendance: Monitored, required, with roll call.

Staff meeting agenda: Long, detailed, fixed, minuscule.

Who talks at staff meetings: One-to-many, mostly top-down; some questions are asked about how to get the job done; details are discussed fully.

Subordinates are promoted: If they appear organized and violate no rules.

What subordinates get praised for: Correctly implementing the process, with little notice taken of the results.

Information that subordinates conceal from him: Organizational transgressions.

Dysfunctional behavior of subordinates: Beating the system to prove that it can't be controlled.

Managing Change

Training practices: Overdone, with excessive focus on details.

Attitude toward change: Resists it because he fears losing control.

Focus of creativity: Throughout the organization; suffocated when it appears.

Attitude toward planning: Over-elaborates to minimize uncertainty and to increase control; takes last year's results and adds some percentage to reach next year's goals.

NOTES

1. The literature provides numerous examples of the ways in which bureaucratic management frustrates and inhibits productivity. For example, Soviet factory managers in the communist regime, according to Berliner, found it impossible to meet their official production quotas without continually violating state laws, industrial regulations, and the party line. See Joseph S. Berliner: *Factory and Manager in the USSR* (Cambridge, Mass.: Harvard University Press, 1957).

    Francis and Stone point out that the same imbalance between (**A**) and (**P**) exist in an American bureaucracy, in which the work ethic conflicts with the tendency toward mindless over-regulation. See Francis, Roy G., and Robert C. Stone: *Service and Procedure in Bureaucracy: A Case Study* (Minneapolis: University of Minnesota Press, 1956).

    As has been stated in the text, subordinates with a (P)roduction orientation soon learn to bypass the Bureaucrat in order to get things done. Blau and Page have documented the presence of informal systems that coexist with the official organization, allowing subordinates to achieve their objectives and to avoid the stifling effects of the exclusive (-A--) management style. See Blau, Peter M.: The Dynamics of Bureaucracy (Chicago: *University of Chicago Press*, 1956).

    See also the discussion of bureaucratic control in Waldo, Dwight, ed.: *Ideas and Issues in Public Administration* (New York: McGraw Hill, 1963), especially Part 1. On the role of the manager as (A)dministrator and (E)ntrepreneur, see Drucker, Peter F., *Management: Tasks, Responsibilities, Practices* (New York: Harper & Row, 1973), pp. 45-57.

2. In government, the (P) and (A) functions are the same. In other words, the (A) actually (P)roduces what the organization exists for. Take a government agency that issues licenses or monitors the health and safety of food service establishments. Its (P) function is to (A)dminister. Of course, this organization will have its traditional (A) roles too: to organize, systematize, and monitor the system.

3. Wouk, Herman: *The Caine Mutiny* (New York: Bantam Doubleday Dell, 1951), p.170.

4. Ibid., p. 131.

5. Ibid., pp. 337-9.

6. "Work expands so as to fill the time available for its completion." C. Northcote Parkinson, *Parkinson's Law: The Pursuit of Progress* (London: John Murray, 1958).

7. Berne, Eric: *Games People Play* (New York: Ballantine, 1996, revised edition).

8. Soros, George, Byron Wien and Krisztina Koenen: *Soros on Soros: Staying Ahead of the Curve* (New York: John Wiley & Sons, 1995).

Chapter 4

The (E)ntrepreneur (PaEi) vs. the Arsonist (- - E -)

In the 1988 film Tucker: *The Man and His Dream*, directed by Frances Ford Coppola and based on a true story, a man named Preston Tucker raised over $20 million in 1948 to start a car company that would challenge the Big Three Detroit car-makers by adding aerodynamic design and safety innovations: Shatterproof glass, a rear engine, seat belts, disc brakes, and fuel injection. A charismatic man, often called a "dreamer" and a "visionary," he raised the money by convincing investors not only that his car would be superior to any other, but that in manufacturing it his tiny company would be able to overcome powerful opposition from the Detroit corporations and the Washington politicians who protected them.

"Whatever you can do, or dream you can do,
begin it."

GOETHE

He actually built 50 cars before the SEC shut down his factory and arrested him for fraud and other violations (he was later acquitted). The car, the Tucker, was an excellent car, and its innovations gradually were adopted as standard by American car-makers. But Tucker and his investors lost everything.

Tucker was an (E)ntrepreneur, but what kind? Let us see.

Seeing through the Fog

Since change is inevitable and constant, the (**E**)ntrepreneurial role is essential to good management. It makes the organization effective in the long run.

The person who performs this (**E**) role analyzes changes in the environment as they affect the organization. He has the imagination and courage to identify strategies in response to such changes.[1]

"The best way to predict the future is to create it."

Peter F. Drucker

Whereas the (**A**)dministrator is given specific plans to (**A**)dminister or decisions to implement, the (**E**)ntrepreneur has to generate his own plan of action. Thus, the manager who performs the (**E**)ntrepreneurial role must have the vision needed to identify possible courses of action and must be willing to act on them. If there is no one to perform the (**E**)ntrepreneurial role in an organization, that organization will eventually lag behind its competitors who are more creative and proactive toward change.

Returning to the "running the railroad" analogy I have used in previous chapters, the (**E**) role would involve deciding which stations to close and which new stations to open, adding or subtracting the number of cars and determining how often the train should stop at each station. The (**E**)ntrepreneur, in other words, points out the direction the organization should take to deal with changing realities.

To be (**E**)ntrepreneurial, a manager must have two major characteristics. He must first of all be creative, able to visualize new directions and devise strategies for adapting the organization to this changing environment. The (**E**)ntrepreneur also has to proact, to prepare the organization to deal with the changes that he has predicted in advance. That means having a willingness to take risks.

A metaphor I find useful for the (**E**) role is "the capability to see through the fog." The creative person will look into the fog and see pieces of information appearing and disappearing, and all at once something clicks. He says, "Aha! I think I know what's out there. I have an idea what it might be and what we might do about it."

The non-creative person waits until the fog lifts, until the sun is shining and it's totally clear, and then says, "Aha, *this* is what I think it might be!" But that person has not added any information or created anything. The creative person, using his imagination, fills in the blanks in the fog.

And yet being creative is not sufficient. Some people are very creative but they are not (**E**)ntrepreneurs. Professors at business schools or business consultants of consulting firms are full of them. If they can teach and advise how to make money, why don't they do it? Because they are *only* creative; they do not have the second characteristic I believe is necessary for an (**E**)ntrepreneur, and that is the willingness to walk *into* the fog, to go and follow the dream: the willingness to take risks.

"Only those who risk going too far
can possibly find out how far one can go."

T. S. Eliot

It is risky to follow a dream. When you get there it may not be what you expected, or there may be dangerous, unforeseen pitfalls along the way.

An (**E**)ntrepreneur, then, is somebody who has a vision, and is willing to take the substantial risk of following this vision. Both qualities are necessary; if a manager is willing to take risks but lacks creativity, he may be more at ease in a Las Vegas casino than in the corporate world. If he is unable to take risks, but is creative, he may end up as a staff person, a consultant, or a business professor – someone who is capable of identifying a course of action but does not undertake it himself.

*"You can't expect to hit the jackpot
if you don't put a few nickels in the machine."*

FLIP WILSON

(E)ntrepreneurship is not confined to the business world. In addition to business (E)ntrepreneurs, who try to exploit the monetary opportunities of the market, there are social (E)ntrepreneurs, who initiate change in the cultural and political sphere, and educational and artistic (E)ntrepreneurs, who initiate activities that satisfy aesthetic needs and generate new ones. All are of tremendous value to society.

THE CREATIVE CONTRIBUTOR (pAEi)

In my previous book How to Solve the Mismanagement Crisis,[2] where I first presented the (PAEI) model, I named the person who performs the (E) role, whose typical code is (paEi), the (E)ntrepreneur. That book was written exactly 30 years ago. Since then, in studying these codes in greater depth, I have changed my mind.

A (paEi) is not quite an (E)ntrepreneur. To be an (E)ntrepreneur, who creates organizations and develops them, one must be strong in the (P) role as well. A focus on (E) alone is not enough.

A person who focuses only on (E), whose (P) orientation is weak – (p) – I now call a Creative Contributor. This is the person who has plenty of ideas – some good, some bad. But he has lots of them, sometimes non-stop. He is like the kid in school whose hand goes up even before he hears the end of the question. He is the person in a meeting who does most of the talking. Whatever solution is proposed, he has another option.

"What is central to business is the joy of creating."

PETER ROBINSON

This person adds energy to the meeting. He is not totally oblivious to what the discussion is about and what the goal is. He is not without some sensitivity to what others are saying, and he is capable of paying attention to details. But without a strong (**P**) focus, he is not the person to say: "Let *me* do it." Without a strong (**P**), he will not be able to build an organization. He will be constantly moving from one idea to the next, without finishing much.

THE (E)NTREPRENEUR (PaEi)

This style knows what he wants and why he wants it. He is creative but in the service of a goal. He has an idea, a purpose, and he can translate that idea into reachable and achievable outcomes. His creativity is focused on how to make that outcome a reality. He is a no-nonsense person, focused and creative. Ideas without results annoy him, and results that are not born out of BIG ideas are a waste of time. That is the (**PaEi**) style.

What happens if it is a (**P-E-**) style: No (**A**) and no (**I**)?

"You look at any giant corporation, and I mean the biggies, and they all started with a guy with an idea, doing it well."

IRVINE ROBBINS, BASKIN-ROBBINS

An executive who attended one of my lectures once pointed out to me that this style is an Arsonist and a Firefighter at the same time. He starts his own fires, then goes to extinguish them. As soon as one fire is out he starts another one. Sometimes he does not wait for one fire to end before he starts a new one. He is his own worst enemy. He creates his own problems, which he then has to solve – but without (**A**) and (**I**) he repeatedly fails at what he starts. The tragedy is that he does not know why he is failing. He is very creative and extremely hardworking. "What am I doing wrong?" he is always asking himself.

A true **(E)**ntrepreneur must be a **(PaEi)** but if he also excels in the **(I)** role – if he is a **(PaEI)** – then he is more than an (E)ntrepreneur. He is a true leader of change. He can visualize what needs to be done and why, and he can motivate people, **(I)**ntegrating them as a team to follow the new direction.

The Arsonist (- - E -)

What happens if the **(E)**ntrepreneurial role is performed exclusively, and the other three roles are not? This manager's efforts would consist entirely of innovating, just charging at any target that appears on his organizational horizon.

If the **(P - - -)**, or Lone Ranger, is also described as a Firefighter, the **(- - E -)** can be called an Arsonist. If the Lone Ranger gets ulcers, the Arsonist causes them.

This is the type of a mismanager I am most familiar with; thus this chapter is somewhat longer than the rest.

Behavior

What are the characteristics that typify an Arsonist? What is important to him?

What we do is not important. That is the domain that interests **(P)**-style managers. *How* we do it is not important either. That is an **(A)** attribute. The Arsonist is concerned with *why not*. With change. With exciting ideas. "What's the difference if it's 50 cars or 50 million?" Preston Tucker (played by Jeff Bridges) asks in the 1988 film. "It's the idea, the dream!"

"You see things as they are and ask, 'Why?'
I dream things as they never were and ask,
'Why not?'"

George Bernard Shaw

When does the Arsonist come to work? Who knows? When does he leave work? Who knows? When do his subordinates come to work? Before him; by the time he comes to work they'd better be there. When do they leave work? Right after him. I've seen vice presidents working for this type of mismanager – it's 7, 8, 9 o'clock at night and they're sitting in their offices watching their nails grow. There's nothing to do, but they can't leave, the boss is still in his office and if they leave, what might happen? The boss might call a meeting: "Drop everything you're doing. Everybody to the meeting room, now." An Arsonist is like an actor, constantly performing. He desperately needs an audience, and he hates to be alone. So he calls meetings frequently and without warning, whenever he has a great new idea.

Here is an extreme case. This is about Frank Lorenzo, who at one time controlled both Continental and Eastern airlines. His vice presidents told me that Frank had an office that overlooked the garage. Whenever his car was parked there they knew he was in the office, watching to see who left ahead of him. Some of the VPs would leave their cars in the parking lot and take a cab home.

Do meetings led by an Arsonist have an agenda? If they do, nobody knows what it is. And even if there is one, he violates it anyway, moving from subject to subject at will or raising subjects that were not scheduled to be discussed. Nevertheless, he expects people to be ready for the meeting. Since the participants never know what topics are going to come up, they arrive at these meetings with their entire file cabinet in their mental suitcase, hoping they're ready to answer any question about anything.

Luckily for them, who does all the talking in these meetings? He does.

Meanwhile, what do the subordinates do? There is a joke that illustrates their behavior. It is an ethnic joke but I don't think it's in bad taste. I hope I am not offending anyone.

Italians are known as great lovers and for their great food and music. But the shortest book ever written is the one that lists Italian military accomplishments. With this background, the joke goes like this:

It is the First World War. The Italian soldiers are in the trenches, ready to attack. Out of the trenches emerges the captain – in a beautiful blue uniform with red sashes, all the decorations, golden epaulets, hat and feathers. He looks dashing. He pulls out his sword and shouts: *"Avaaaaaaantiiiiiii!"*

What do the soldiers do? They clap hands and shout: "Bra-vooooooo!" But nobody gets out of the trenches.

Why? Because, like an Arsonist, the captain doesn't say, "Attack in this new direction and stop the previous direction!" He says, "At-tack in *this* direction, and also *that* direction, that *other* direction, and that fourth direction." So what can the soldiers do? They stay in the trenches and shout *"Bravooooooo!"* And when they're asked, "Are you attacking?" their typical answer is "We're working on it."

In an organization managed by an Arsonist, who is it who will actually get out of the trenches and attack? It is usually those who have just been hired. These new subordinates have not yet had the experience of running around and getting nowhere. Those who have been around for a while sit and wait: Maybe the boss did not really mean it. Maybe he'll change his mind. Experienced subordinates know enough to wait and see whether the idea was just an idea or a true, honest-to-goodness decision that will survive the test of time. So they do little, simply waiting, while the Arsonist hyperventilates.

Picture an organization as an axle. There is a big wheel at one end (in English, "a big wheel" even has a corporate meaning) and a small wheel at the other end. When the big wheel makes one revolution, the small wheel must turn many times. If the big wheel is an Arsonist, he will frequently change direction while the smaller wheels are still in motion. Eventually the gears of the smaller wheels are stripped and the axle breaks down. The big wheel is left spinning alone.

So eventually, when the Arsonist changes direction, the experi-enced staff people have learned to say, "Bravo, we're on it!" but they don't really take any action. They watch from the sidelines, calling out to each other, "Here he comes! There he goes!" But they don't move. They know that too many priorities equal no priorities; all directions equal no direction. They sit, clap their hands, and show support – because if they don't they risk being considered obstructionist or disloyal. But they do little else.

It is not surprising, then, that an Arsonist is always saying, "I don't understand what's going on. I have all these beautiful ideas, these visions of opportunities, and my subordinates are constantly 'working on it.' But not enough is being achieved."

He doesn't realize that he himself is responsible for the breakdown. Instead, he thinks, "Somebody must be undermining my efforts." He becomes paranoid and looks for someone to blame.

Stalin, for example, was a big **(E)**. (I do not know about the other roles.) He had paranoid tendencies; periodically he would execute a whole bunch of even his closest friends and gather a new group of subordinates whom he would eventually lose trust in and execute.

This tendency to need enemies is part of the culture among **(E)**-oriented ethnic groups. Take the Jewish people, who excel in **(E)**. There is a joke about a Jew who was stranded alone on an island for many years. When he was located, his rescuers saw that he had built two synagogues. "Why two?" they asked.

"And whom would I criticize?" he answered.

This is an **(E)**'s way of feeling in control. All of the mismanagement styles crave control, but they manifest that craving in different ways. The **(P - - -)** tries to maintain control by doing everything himself. An **(- A - -)** creates a system of rules and policies that nobody dares to violate. An **(- - - I)** establishes control by insisting that everyone agree. An **(- - E -)** seizes control by being the one to have all the ideas and make all the decisions; whoever disagrees with him or is less than enthusiastic in his support becomes an enemy. "If you are not for me, you are against me," is a typical **(E)** attitude.

These are all extremes, and the result of this exaggerated single-role performance is that the **(P)** becomes a Lone Ranger, the **(A)** becomes a Bureaucrat, the **(I)** becomes a SuperFollower, and the **(E)** becomes an Arsonist.

"And just how long have people accused you of being a 'take charge' type?"

An Arsonist is usually very likable, because he is stimulating, enterprising, and full of energy. Working for him can be exciting – until you figure out that no matter what you do the Arsonist will find fault with it. Why? Because his priorities are continually changing and nobody can keep up with them, no matter what they achieve. The Arsonist keeps moving the goal line, which means that his subordinates inevitably fail to satisfy him and feel like failures. Before you've completed one project, he wants to know why you haven't made any progress on a new one.

The Arsonist likes to witness the furor that his initiatives cause. He likes an atmosphere of urgency and is delighted when his subordinates are rushing in and out, trying to cope with the emergencies he's created.

"There's never any talent without a little stain of madness."

Jean-Louis Trintignant

Under such managers, projects are always being completed under pressure. The staff is forced to work overtime and crucial details remain in a state of flux right up to the last minute. That is why artistic directors do not decide what the repertoire for the coming year is going to be until it is time to go to print or publishers have to impose deadlines on authors who, without such a deadline, would be writing and rewriting their books for years.

(E)s need to have boundaries imposed from the outside, because they cannot do it themselves. Imposing boundaries curtails their creativity and sense of boundless possibilities. For an (E), endings are like a death. As long as something can be improved, it is alive. So an (E) hates boundaries – and those who set them – with a passion. The more creative they are, the more miserable and victimized they feel when they have to function within any kind of limits.

Attention to Detail

Details are the Arsonist's Achilles' heel. The (- -E-) tends to ignore details; he works with a big brush on a wide canvas, as if he were looking down from 40,000 feet at a topographical map. For an (- - E -), a million is somewhere between 700,000 and a million and a half–while for an (- A - -), 999,999 is not the same as a million. You can see why (E)'s and (A)'s don't usually get along. An (A) invariably accuses the (E) of being a liar, while the (E) is convinced that the (A) is not awfully bright.

On the Native Americans' medicine wheel, which I mentioned in Chapter 2, the (- - E -) style corresponds to an eagle, soaring thousands of feet above the ground. From up there, everything looks simple; after all, with one movement of its wings it can fly from one boulder to another. The eagle cannot comprehend that down on the ground, in order to move from one location to another, you may have to hike up and down mountains and canyons.

"The road to Hell is paved
with good intentions."

16TH-CENTURY PROVERB

Negativity

Arsonists act out of emotion and nervous energy; very often it's negative energy. They have a huge need to build something new, which often means destroying what's already in place. In order to "own" their idea, they feel they have to start from scratch or change what is there, even if it is more than adequate already.

If you ask an (- **A**- -), "How's it going?" he'll tell you, "It's under control, it's fine, just don't make waves." If you ask a (**P** - - -), he'll brush you off: "I have no time. I don't know. Too busy. I'll tell you later." If you ask an (- - - **I**), "How are you feeling?" he'll say, "How are you feeling?"

If you ask an (- - **E** -) executive, "How's it going?" he'll immediately start thinking about what *isn't* fine. If you ask him, "How am I doing?" he'll tell you, "You're doing OK, *but* let me tell you how you can improve." Why? Because if everything is wonderful, how will he find the energy to tear it down? And yet he *must* tear it down in order to build something new that's his. By definition, he must find something wrong with everything.

Here is a joke that makes that point:

What does a waitress ask the table of old Jewish ladies?

"Is *anything* all right?"

The (**E**)'s tendency to be hypercritical makes working for him very difficult. An (**E**)'s subordinates are always on the verge of quitting, and the (**E**) often has to bribe them to get them to stay. He overpays them; he might give them a car and use of the corporate jet or send them on paid vacations – to keep them working while he continues to criticize the hell out of them.

Motivation

Economists believe that what drives (**E**)ntrepreneurs is money, profits. My experience and insight have led me to believe otherwise. In
reality, many of the (- - **E** -)s I talk to don't even know how much
money they have–they've lost count. They cannot buy more shoes;
they cannot buy more airplanes. I have clients who don't know what
to do with their money: They have airplanes, yachts, three or four
or five or six houses; and yet they keep right on building or buying
another company. Some of them do it even though they might be
risking everything they've built.

"If you want to be happy, be."

LEO TOLSTOY

What is it that motivates them? I don't believe it's money. I think
there are two elements that drive the Arsonist: his ego, and an intense
fear of death. The (**E**) fears oblivion and craves immortality. He is
obsessed with the need to leave something behind after his death, so
he keeps building bigger and bigger monuments. This explains the
constant, restless activity.

Behind this kind of brinkmanship, *bravado*, impulsive risk-taking,
and out-on-a-limb leadership, there may be a mild form of manic
depression, or bi-polar disorder. Some psychiatrists have theorized
that some form of the disorder, characterized by manic highs and
depressive lows, might contribute to the creative, risk-taking behavior
of (**E**)ntrepreneurs like Steve Jobs and Bill Gates.

In his book Moodswing: *Dr. Fieve on Depression*,[3] Dr. Ronald R.
Fieve describes a subtype of bipolar disorder – hypomania–in which
the person has a "genetic predisposition to creative high moods." As
examples, he names Ted Turner and former chairman of ITT Har-
old Geenen, who used to regularly work through the night into the
morning hours and habitually carried ten suitcases around with him
instead of a briefcase.

A person with this condition, Fieve writes, "has a tremendous advantage as long as he doesn't overextend and start showing poor judgment by going too high" – i.e., becoming an Arsonist.

Other executives, leaders, and (E)ntrepreneurs who have acknowledged having the disorder include editor and publisher Frances Lear;[4] Canadian real estate magnate Robert Campeau[5] and Canadian publisher Pierre Péladeau;[6] and financiers J.P. Morgan[7], John Mulheren,[8] and Murray Pezim.[9]

COMMUNICATION

An Arsonist assumes that silence equals agreement. That's a source of miscommunication, especially when dealing with an (A) type, for whom silence equals *dis*agreement.

Typically, an (- - E -) goes to an (A) and suggests some change; the (A) does not say a word. The (- - E -) leaves the room. If you ask him, "How did it go?" he says, "Fantastic. He's totally sold on the idea. He didn't say a word."

Later on, when the (- - E -) asks for a progress report, the (A) responds, "What are you talking about? I never agreed to that idea."

The (- - E -) is furious. "Why didn't you speak up? You didn't say a word. You gave me the impression that you agreed when in reality you did not agree. How can I trust you? You are sabotaging me! You are passive-aggressive! You don't tell me the truth! You communicate one thing and mean something else!"

He might fire the (A) for being an untrustworthy obstructionist, a saboteur. The (A) will go home, bewildered and shocked, and tell his spouse, "He fired me. I don't know why. I didn't say a word."

Working with (A)s, I had to learn to frequently stop and ask them: "Do you agree?" With an (E), of course, that is unnecessary; they let me know immediately and vocally when they disagree.

If I do not ask the (A)s, their silence might confuse me. I am an (E) myself, and thus I, too, used to assume agreement when there was silence, when in reality the opposite was true.

Coherence

Because they create on the run, Arsonists often contradict themselves: the mouth is talking, the mind is working, but there isn't necessarily a connection. An (- - **E** -) often says, "It's too late to disagree with me; I've already changed my mind." He starts with one angle, and changes to another angle and then a third angle, and eventually you can't follow what he's saying.

"If you can't convince them, confuse them."

HARRY S. TRUMAN

Yet not being understood upsets and offends an Arsonist, and he can react with unbelievable hostility. Why? Because he's really upset with himself; he doesn't understand why he is unable to adequately communicate what he wants to say. He becomes hostile with those people who haven't understood him, deciding that it's all their fault. Here is a typical (**E**) expression: "It is difficult to soar like an eagle when you are surrounded by turkeys."

When a small child cannot explain himself, he might start screaming and crying and banging the table with his fist. An Arsonist is like that small child. Some (**E**) executives, particularly Arsonists, can be outrageously vulgar and abusive in their anger.

"What you need is to organize your thoughts," I tell (**E**)s. "It's very difficult for others to understand you until you understand yourself first. Sit. Take a piece of paper, and write down what it is that you want to say. Then read it. Probably you will disagree with what you wrote. So rewrite it. Continue until you feel comfortable with what you've written, and then you'll be ready to explain it to others."

They never follow this advice. They hate to put anything in writing, if they can help it.

A pad and pencil is an essential tool for any executive, of any style. But the probability of an (- - **E** -) actually using them is very low. Arsonists don't like to put anything in writing. If you ask them, for the record, to summarize in writing what was discussed and agreed to, you probably won't get it, because Arsonists don't want to be boxed in. They want the freedom to change their minds.

Thus, you should never assign an (**E**) to record the minutes of a meeting. In the process of transcribing his notes, he might easily decide that he has a better idea than the one the group arrived at; and the minutes he produces will have little resemblance to everyone else's recollections of what took place. In any case, he probably was not listening carefully to what was going on. He was too busy listening to his own ideas to open his mind and hear other people's contributions.

When an Arsonist speaks, people often don't know whether he is deciding or simply thinking out loud. Sometimes the subordinates believe the boss has made a decision, so they begin to implement it and then discover it wasn't a decision at all – it was just an idea. They get penalized for acting without authorization. Then, of course, the next time the (- - **E** -) thinks out loud, his subordinates remember the last episode and don't act, thinking that this, too, is just an idea. The Arsonist gets equally upset – but this time because his staff *doesn't* implement his instructions, which actually did reflect a final decision.

After a few fiascos, the employees begin to feel there is no way they can win. No matter what they do, they're going to be humiliated for something. They are damned if they act and damned if they don't.

In Australia, I once worked with a CEO who was an Arsonist. One day as we were walking down the corridor, this CEO said to his vice president for manufacturing – a (**P**)-type – "How come we don't have a factory in Brisbane?"

The manufacturing VP said, "You think we should have one?"

The CEO said, "Why don't we?"

What do you think happened next? The VP behaved exactly as you would expect a (**P**) to behave: He started preparing to build a manufacturing facility in Brisbane. But when the CEO found out, he was very angry. "Why the hell are we going to build a factory in Brisbane?"

"But you said you wanted it."

"I was just asking you why we *don't* have one. I didn't tell you to have one!"

An Arsonist habitually works on the "why don't we?" principle: "Why don't we do this?" "Why don't we do that?" But what is a mere question for an (- - **E** -) is assumed to be a decision by his subordinates, especially the (**P**)s. This miscommunication can be dangerous because an Arsonist does not know how to bite his tongue; he just lets go. An (**E**)s tendency, especially if he is an Arsonist, is to talk and talk. But in addition to creating confusion, Arsonists lose credibility that way, because the more they talk the more they contradict themselves and go in circles. Other people begin to discount their opinions.

I have had clients who needed a "translator," somebody who understands him, who can see where he is coming from and where he is going, and interpret for others what he is saying.

What is the other skill necessary for communication? Listening. And of all the four types, the (- - **E** -) is the worst listener. Why? Because he's full of ideas and it's so easy to trigger more. Anything you say might trigger a chain of thought in him, and while he's developing the little seed you planted, he's so busy listening to himself that he doesn't hear the rest of what you say. In fact, he perceives others' talking as an irritating distraction.

"When you speak, you can't listen.
When you don't listen, you can't learn."

BERNARD LIND

Sometimes, what is not being said can be more important than what is being said. (**E**)s do not understand that. An (**I**) grasps that principle intuitively; he can hear and interpret silence. He can tell you, "Jim did not say such and such, but he wanted to, and here is why he didn't. ..." (**I**)s know exactly what is *not* being said and *why* it's not being said and *who* is not saying it. Not (**E**)s; they are mostly busy listening to themselves.

Impulsive; expressive

In conversation, the Arsonist is emotional and expressive. In (E)-oriented cultures such as Israel or Greece, everyone talks simultaneously, and a standing joke in such countries is that the first person who stops to take a breath loses the argument.

"Nothing is quite so annoying as to have someone go right on talking when you're interrupting."

BITS AND PIECES, VOLUME C, NO. 12

This communication behavior closely resembles the psychiatric definition of the narcissist. The (- - **E** -), like the narcissist, is in love with his own work and ideas – with himself.

I am neither a psychologist nor a psychiatrist, but in reading a profile of the narcissist by Michael Maccoby in the *Harvard Business Review*,[10] I saw perfect parallels between the narcissistic style and the (- - **E** -) style of management. Below I have summarized some of his relevant points.

Maccoby claims, and I agree with him, that narcissistic leaders "are gifted and creative strategists who see the *big picture* and find meaning in the risky challenge of changing the world and leaving behind a *legacy*."

They are, claims Maccoby: charmers, inspire people, are independent and not easily impressed, driven to gain power and glory. They are charismatic, want to learn everything about everything, and can become unrealistic dreamers.

Maccoby, who is a psychiatrist, claims that narcissistic leaders think that they are invincible: "As he expands, he listens even less to words of caution and advice.... Rather than try to persuade those who disagree with him, he feels justified in ignoring them...."

"If you don't agree with me, it means you haven't been listening."

SAM MARKEWICH

Narcissists, claims Maccoby, "dominate meetings with subordinates.... The result is sometimes flagrant risk-taking that can lead to catastrophe.... Because of their independence and aggressiveness, they are constantly looking out for enemies, sometimes degenerating into paranoia when they are under extreme stress."

Narcissists, says Maccoby, are emotionally isolated, highly distrustful, ... extraordinarily sensitive, shun emotions as a whole, typically keep others at arm's length ... and are uncomfortable with other people expressing their (feelings) – especially their negative feelings. They find intimacy to be difficult. They easily lose their temper with subordinates although they are quite dependent on their followers–they need affirmation, and preferably adulation.

Narcissists "listen only for the kind of information they seek... They cannot tolerate dissent. In fact, they can be extremely abrasive with employees who doubt them or with subordinates who are tough enough to fight back.... Perceived threats can trigger rage.... although [they] often say that they want teamwork, what that means in practice is that they want a group of yes-men. As the more independent-minded players leave or are pushed out, succession becomes a particular problem..."

"He is a self-made man, and he worships his creator."

JOHN BRIGHT ABOUT DISRAELI

Dr. Maccoby says that narcissists, type (**E**) in my parlance, are often more interested in controlling others than in knowing and disciplining themselves. They don't want to change – and as long as they are successful, they don't think they have to. Their lack of empathy and their extreme independence makes it difficult to mentor them. Most narcissists prefer "mentors" they can control.

"We always weaken whatever we exaggerate."

JEAN FRANCOIS DE LAHARPE

Precision

The (- - **E** -) habitually exaggerates. He favors words like "never," "always," "impossible." It's one method of overpowering an opponent in argument; the Arsonist exaggerates in order to really push his ideas through.

When an (- - **E** -) says, "We sold a million-dollar contract," and an (A), who takes what he hears literally, asks: "Where is the contract?" the (- - **E** -) might respond: "It's coming."

"So, we don't have it yet!" the (A) says with some irritation.

"But we will. It's coming. They said so."

"But we do not actually *have* it!" the (**A**) almost screams.

In bureaucratic organizations, where the (**A**) culture dominates, (**E**)s of all kinds are distrusted. They are considered to be manipulative, compulsive liars, whose signature you'd better have on the dotted line if you expect anything to happen. Eventually, an (**A**) culture will gets rid of its (**E**)s, thus accelerating its own demise. It rejects what it needs most to survive, because it does not know how to handle a conflicting style.

Decision-Making

In a company managed by an Arsonist, Monday mornings are dangerous. Why? Because over the weekend the Arsonist has had time to think. Monday morning comes and what happens? New directions, new priorities, new goals, new objectives.

Another dangerous day is when the Arsonist returns from a trip, because sitting on that plane with nothing to do for three hours, he has had a series of brainstorms. By the time he arrives, everybody's whispering: "Get ready, here he comes!"

Because, not in spite of, the numerous ideas, priorities, and goals that he generates, not much happens in a company run by an Arsonist. The Arsonist doesn't like to finalize anything; everything can be improved; even in mid-change anything might be changed again in yet another, "better" direction. Everything is open-ended.

Every idea leads to another idea: Subject A reminds him of subject B which reminds him of subject C – until before you know it, people are asking, "What happened? We had an agenda of ten items, and we hardly covered the first one."

An Arsonist cannot stay with one subject. His decision-making process is mercurial, constantly moving to a related idea. He does not understand that by adding an idea, he's diminishing the value of other ideas because there's a limit to how much one person or one company can handle.

"Why not go out on a limb? Isn't that where the fruit is?"

FRANK SCULLY

(- - **E** -)s have difficulty discerning what is a "need-to" versus what is only a "nice-to." For them, *everything* is a "need-to"; their desires have the urgency of needs. But the perceptual handicap that renders them unable to discriminate between one and the other also makes them incapable of allocating the company's resources according to their priorities. When a company has 122 priorities, it has no priorities.

When I work with an (- - **E** -), my first task is to identify all his goals: "Let's accumulate all the things we want. Now, let's identify which are the things we *need* to have and which are the things it's *nice to* have. Then, out of what we need to have, let's prioritize, give each goal some weight." I usually whittle down this list into three to five driving forces. All the others are "nice-to."

Throughout this process, I'm forcing the (- - **E** -) to discriminate. For an (- - **E** -), it is extremely painful to do this exercise. He suffers. He has real difficulty deciding what *not* to do. He wants it all. An Arsonist hates to make choices: he wants everything; behaviorally he refuses to acknowledge that time and resources have limits.

"If the facts don't fit the theory, change the facts."

ALBERT EINSTEIN

Nor does he measure the cost of his plans against their value. An Arsonist, to misquote Oscar Wilde, "knows the value of everything, but the cost of nothing." An (- - **E** -) is always busy planning, then promoting, the brilliant innovations he's going to make. But how much will they cost? What repercussions will there be? "These are details," he'll shrug. "Don't bug me with the details." This is why an Arsonist can build a big company and lose it overnight.

Consistency

When an Arsonist sets a policy, he is often the first one to break it. For example, I had a client whose Internet company incubator was failing. The decision was made not to start another company for a period of three years, unless investment money became available. The very next week, this company's Arsonist began a new start-up. Why? Because the concept excited him. He "wanted it badly." It was "the best thing since sliced bread," it was "an opportunity that could not be passed up," etc., and we should all trust his judgment.

Perception of Reality

Arsonists often behave as if what they *want* is what actually is. They have a hard time accepting reality.

"If you can dream it, you can do it."

WALT DISNEY

An (- - **E** -) will say, for example, "Our company is the leader of the industry."

"But we *aren't*," you might argue.

"Yes, but we *should* be," he will respond. "We are doing everything possible: we are doing the R&D, we are developing the market." In other words: "Since I *want* it, it *is*." He confuses reality with the reality he wishes to have.

This can be a great advantage; many of history's most successful (**E**)ntrepreneurs shared that trait. As George Bernard Shaw once said, "Reasonable people adapt to their environment; unreasonable people try to adapt their environment to themselves. Thus, all progress is the result of the efforts of unreasonable men."

An (**E**)ntrepreneur fits perfectly Shaw's description of the "unreasonable" man. Take David Ben Gurion, the first prime minister of Israel. When Ben Gurion was asked, "Do you believe in miracles?" he answered, "We plan for them." In other words, when you look at an (- - **E** -)'s project planning document (assuming there is anything in writing), somewhere along the PERT (Program Evaluation Review Technique) diagram an item will appear that states: "Here we will have a miracle." And they rely on it. Theodor Herzl, the founder of modern Zionism, said something similar about the prospects of a Jewish state: "If you want it, it will not be a fairy tale!"

"Once you make a decision,
the universe conspires to make it happen."

RALPH WALDO EMERSON

Deep in his mind, an (- - **E** -) believes, "I am going to do what I want to do, and don't you worry, everything will turn out right." It is this optimistic and non-realistic streak that makes an (**E**) have the courage to start companies. The practical (**P**)s and risk-averse (**A**)s do not start companies: they look at what is, measure the costs of getting what they *want*, and decide against trying. (**E**)s do what they *want* – *despite* the fact that they are relying on unrealistic odds.

When you hear an Arsonist use the word *should*, pay particular attention. *Should* is supposed to mean that you analyzed the inputs and outputs and compared them, the cost versus the value, and then made a decision that is an optimal one. You want to be sure that the cost does not exceed the value, that the value justifies the costs, before you approve. But if you carefully analyze what the Arsonist is saying, you often realize that the word *should* actually means that's what he *wants*. What he *wants* is the way it *should* be. He only considers value and opportunities, downplaying the importance of costs. He wants something because he wants it, although it may be the wrong thing to do or the wrong time to do it.

"A pessimist sees a difficulty in every opportunity; an optimist sees opportunity in every difficulty."

WINSTON CHURCHILL

Alan Bond was once one of the richest men in Australia. He owned many companies, from beer companies to TV stations – but by the time he went bankrupt for the third time, he owed billions to the banks and had to go to prison for some serious violations of securities laws. He was working only with *want*, not paying attention to *should*. He saw only opportunities, no threats.

I knew Alan personally, and saw him try to do too much too fast, too many times. That's another Arsonist trait: Their measurement of time is skewed, unless they compensate by using what I call a "bias multiple" to judge time realistically and appropriately.

Let me explain that. Picture the (- - **E** -) as that eagle I mentioned earlier, flying over the mountains and seeing the big picture but not the small details. From up there, moving is very easy. But on the ground, traveling over boulders and canyons and mountains, the trip is much more difficult, slower, and sometimes not even possible.

"Men do not stumble over mountains, but over molehills."

CONFUCIUS

Now, the higher up the Arsonist is in the organization, the more repercussions his slightest move will have below. That's the bias multiple: If he is 10,000 feet up, he believes something can be done in a week–no problem! – while in reality it might take six weeks. That is a bias multiple of six. The higher he goes, the higher his bias multiple becomes, because he sees fewer of the complexities and details of implementation.

Because he is bored by details, the Arsonist's attitude and preferences are to decentralize. But it's equally important for him to maintain control of the decision-making process. The result is a catch-22 for his subordinates. They are *expected* to decide – as long as their decisions coincide with the decision *he* would have taken. But they don't know what they'd need to know to make a decision his way. Only he knows, and he keeps changing his mind. For his subordinates, that decision is a moving target, and the result is paralysis.

Please note that, like the Bureaucrat who is so focused on efficiency that he creates an inefficient bureaucracy, the Arsonist is so focused on change that he creates paralysis.

IMPLEMENTING

The Arsonist's primary interest is not in *whether* the job is done, nor even in *how* it is done, but rather in whether it *should* be done – which really means whether he *wants* it done. He cares about the process, the novelty – not necessarily the results. He is interested in the *why not*, whereas the Lone Ranger is interested in the *what* and the Bureaucrat in the *how*. The Arsonist does not really want to work. He wants to be challenged and have fun.

As a result, many (- - **E** -)s "manage with a pointing finger." That's a Hebrew expression, meaning that they simply point with their finger and say: "Do this, do that." They don't get involved with implementation.

"There are no unrealistic goals, only unrealistic time frames."

LARRY PRESSER

Because they hold everyone but themselves responsible for implementation, they tend to speak with exaggerated authority. It's sometimes said of this type of manager that he is "seldom right but never in doubt."

The Arsonist typically will develop fantastic ideas and then expect others to figure out how to implement them. If he is pressed for specifics, he gets annoyed.

A joke told by Will Rogers illustrates this. During World War I, the Navy called in a consultant to advise them on how to cope with German submarines. The consultant studied the situation and recommended that the ocean be heated to a temperature of 180 degrees. This would force the German submarines to surface, where they could be easily found and destroyed.

The Navy thought this was a fine idea but did not know how to heat the ocean. When questioned on this matter, the consultant replied, "I'm a planner. These are details. It is your job to worry about the details."

*"Nothing is impossible to a man who does not
have to do it himself."*

A.H. Weiler

Dreamers

Just as they have difficulty facing reality during the decision-making process, Arsonists cling to their dreams even after they become implementation nightmares. They refuse to wake up.

The philosopher George Santayana once said that when you lose sight of your aim while redoubling your efforts, you have become a fanatic. And that's what happens to (- - **E** -)s: If they double their efforts and do not succeed, they will quadruple them, until eventually they're focused on winning instead of on achieving the original goal. They insist it has to work. Why? "Because I *want* it to, and since I *want* it to it *should* be." In a business organization, such leadership can lead to bankruptcy, while in the political arena it can have even more disastrous repercussions.

Hitler was an example of a fanatical (**E**) type. By the end of World War II, he had totally lost his grip on reality and was commanding his army by measuring distances on a map with his fingers. He refused to even consider the problems and details of implementation. But he was trying to win the war with 12-year-old soldiers.

Support people fear the Arsonist because he's always bursting with ideas and never seems to notice how difficult or costly the implementation might be. He is extremely aggressive and monopolizes decision-making meetings. When the meeting is over, those who were in the room are bewildered or resentful or both. The new plan may be totally unrealistic, but all they can do is hope he'll forget about it or try to find plausible explanations for why it isn't getting done.

TEAM-BUILDING

Arsonists do not play well with others.

In the 1970s, I was in Peru consulting with the prime minister there. I had a free afternoon, so I went to the beach. In front of me was a beautiful sand castle some child had made.

Out of the corner of my eye, I saw another kid approaching. I knew what he was going to do: He was going to knock over the castle. That's a typical Arsonist. You already have a gorgeous castle – but, "No, no, no, it's not *my* castle." He needs to break it down and build his own castle.

If you give an (- - **E** -) an idea, he might say, "No, I don't agree with you," but then next week he will give you back the same idea, rephrased, as if he'd thought of it himself. That makes people very upset.

Arsonists love change even though it creates conflict and chaos. In fact, very smart Arsonists actually encourage disagreements so that they can spot dissenters and destroy them.

Here's an example: In 1991, I was invited by the prime minister of Serbia, Prof. Zelenovic, to advise the Yugoslav government on how to prevent the breakdown of its federation, which was falling apart. I came to the conclusion that the problem was not Croatia or Slovenia, which were both trying to secede, but Kosovo. Kosovo was very underdeveloped and was costing the Yugoslav federation about $1.5 billion in aid annually. Most of this money was coming from forced contributions from the resources of Croatia and Slovenia, which had no emotional connection to Kosovo. Serbia, however, considered Kosovo the birthplace of its nation: "This is our Jerusalem," I was told.

Eventually, both Croatia and Slovenia did secede from Yugoslavia, in protest against Serbian dominance and then-President Slobodan Milosevic's unilateral decision to continue supporting Kosovo financially. After the secession, Serbia was forced to pay for aid to Kosovo by itself.

In a private meeting with Milosevic and Zelenovic, I advised Milosevic to emancipate Kosovo, to let it go and invest the $1.5 billion in Serbia instead. "Kosovo is the gangrene of Serbia," I told Milosevic. "It's endangering Serbia in the long run. It's using resources that Serbia needs for its own development. And why support and develop a region whose people are enemies of the Serbs to begin with?"

Milosevic said, "I think you are right," and he asked Zelenovic if he agreed. Zelenovic said, "Yes, I think he is right." Milosevic instructed Zelenovic to work on a plan to set new borders, hold a referendum for self-determination, encourage the Kosovo Albanians to vote for secession, and move the Serbian population out of Kosovo. I was even sent to meet with the U.S. ambassador to Yugoslavia, Warren Zimmerman, to solicit support for the plan. But Milosevic never called me again. And soon thereafter, he fired Zelenovic.

I call that "watering the field, watching the weeds grow, then cutting off their heads." That was Tito's strategy, too: he identified opposition *by encouraging* it; then he imprisoned those who had voiced dissent.

In retrospect, it is clear that Milosevic never intended to implement the strategy I recommended. What he was really trying to do was find out whether Zelenovic, his prime minister, agreed with him or with me. By encouraging Zelenovic to agree with me, he was able to confirm his suspicion, so Zelenovic was dismissed.

Needs

(- - **E** -)s are often considered to be narcissistic, self-centered troublemakers. They always act like they know best. They are constantly giving advice and can hardly stand to take it. Their behavior is driven by a tremendous need for approval and applause. My theory is that they are really love-deficient, and are so obsessively creative because they want to be accepted and admired by others.

When I ask about the childhoods of the (- - **E** -) executives I work with, I invariably find that they were isolated for part of their lives: Tom Monaghan, the founder of Domino's Pizza, was an orphan. Anita Roddick, who founded The Body Shop, was an immigrant, a fish out of water in her environment. Or take me: In World War II, I was hiding from the Germans in the mountains of Albania, with no friends but the chickens.

So Arsonists have a strong need to fit in. They want to be accepted and even applauded, and the way they achieve that is by being creative. The danger is that if they get disapproval instead, they become hostile and sometimes destructive. If an Arsonist loses control of a company he built, he might actually kill it, like an animal that eats its own young. And that's what eventually happened with Milosevic in Yugoslavia.

"Temper is what gets most of us into trouble.
Pride is what keeps us there."

BITS AND PIECES, VOLUME C NO. 12

Approval of Others

The Arsonist more or less approves of the Lone Ranger, since the (**P- - -**) works hard for the organization, but his approval is qualified because the Lone Ranger never has time to listen to the Arsonist, who desperately needs an audience. The Arsonist and the Bureaucrat are constantly at odds. The Arsonist gets along very well with the SuperFollower – a style we will meet in the next chapter – because the SuperFollower knows exactly how to cater to his ego.

Managing Staff

It takes a very strong person to work with an Arsonist, and yet (**- - E -**)s surround themselves with weak people. Why? Because an (**- - E -**) has to win every argument, and weak subordinates will never challenge him.

If the Lone Ranger's subordinates are gofers and the subordinates of the Bureaucrat are yes-yes men, the typical subordinates of the

Arsonist are claque. Claques (it's a French word; in Mexico they are called *palleros*) are the hired hands in opera houses who are paid to start clapping when a singer ends an aria, to encourage the rest of the audience to applaud as well.

Members of a claque are required to agree with the Arsonist's ideas, at least in public. An Arsonist views a public disagreement the way an opera singer might view a heckler who boos when he is at his high C. The Arsonist holds grudges and will not easily forget this threat to his ego.

The result is that the Arsonist invariably receives tumultuous applause, but it isn't real. As soon as these hired hands leave the opera house, they say to each other, "That was terrible!" And in corporations, they commiserate with each other: "My God, there he goes, charging full-speed ahead all over again, taking risks that can destroy us. How are we going to get him off charging again?" They start out in their jobs working hard to catch up, but eventually they learn that it's pointless to put in all that effort because the Arsonist is going to change direction anyway, or unilaterally lift the bar higher.

The Arsonist's subordinates also learn, however, not to reject his plans outright, because he will interpret a rejection of his ideas as a rejection of himself. Thus, the subordinates are in a bind: they see no use in trying to achieve the Arsonist's goals, yet they cannot refuse to accept them. Their way out is to accept the tasks but do very little about them. They come up with creative excuses instead, trying to appear cooperative without actually cooperating.

A middle-management editor at a newspaper in New Jersey described one Arsonist editor-in-chief as follows: "He loved to pit his employees against one another (he called it "healthy competition"), and he seemed to enjoy the chaos that resulted whenever he reassigned people to different positions and even different departments – which he did so often that it was almost impossible to master your job before you were switched over to something else. It was like playing "musical chairs." But if you protested, you were demoted at the next opportunity.

"His excitement about his own ideas seemed to be contagious to those above him, however, and he often convinced the publisher to make changes that were extremely time-consuming to achieve. He would give the publisher unrealistic expectations, promising immediate results, and then accuse us of betrayal when the impossible failed to happen.

"You could never go to him with a problem, because he would humiliate you for not being able to solve it, and then, in attempting to solve it himself, he would come up with six or seven new ideas he wanted to add on, or he'd change his mind entirely – and you would leave his office with many more problems than you'd had going in.

"If you had an idea of your own, he would dismiss it rudely, then bring it up a few weeks later as if he'd just thought of it himself.

"He expected his subordinates to be in the office seven days a week, 18 hours a day. He never had a nice word to say about the sections I'd produce; he was just happy to see that I was there working even at 1 a.m.

"He tortured quite a few people into quitting the newspaper," this former editor concluded, "and many people – I was one of them – were so demoralized that they abandoned the newspaper business entirely."

The CEO of one company that I consulted with would actually call people on Christmas Eve and Christmas morning to discuss business. He once called one of his vice presidents on this man's wedding anniversary and said, "I am flying to Washington on the corporate jet. Come join me; I want to discuss something with you. Then you can take a commercial flight back."

Whenever the Arsonist is in sight, his subordinates pretend to be busy with his current pet project. If he pokes his head into a subordinate's office and asks, "How are you doing?" the typical answer is "Busy, busy, busy." (If you don't look busy enough, the Arsonist will assign more work.) But if the (- - **E** -) does not follow up about an assignment or leaves the office, the subordinates drop it. Since Arsonists usually don't follow up on assignments they give, people listen, give the impression that they will do as requested and do it enthusiastically, when in reality they put the task on the back burner. That is why I repeatedly warn (**E**)s: "What gets done in a company is not what is *expected*, but what is *inspected*." (**E**)s manage by expectations (which are ever-changing) so they are always feeling disillusioned, disappointed, and betrayed.

A member of an Arsonist's claque leads a double life. On one hand he's cheering at all the meetings, but outside the office he's lying on the psychiatrist's couch, moaning, "I don't know what to do." He frequently has marital problems, because he's on call for this boss 365 days a year, 24 hours a day.

Because of his faulty bias multiple, an Arsonist cannot accurately envision the difficulties his subordinates will have in implementing his plans. If he wants to do something that might take a year, he believes it can be done in a month. When a month passes and little progress has been made, he becomes frustrated and angry and believes his subordinates are dragging their feet.

"A person is about as big as the things that make him angry."

BITS AND PIECES, VOLUME C NO. 12

This defective judgment contributes to the Arsonist's paranoid tendencies. He really believes that somebody is screwing up. He won't acknowledge that part of the problem is his continual change of direction, which his subordinates react to by not knowing what to do or by deciding to do nothing, since he's going to change his mind anyway. He is his own worst enemy: Changing direction, confusing people, abusing his subordinates. This makes the organization relatively ineffective and inefficient – so naturally the Arsonist will look for a scapegoat.

As a matter of fact, my experience with Arsonist clients is that they always have a "villain on duty." They believe that because of this person, things are not moving right or fast or well. "So why don't you fire him?" I ask. Then I find out that this love-hate dance has been going on for years. He complains, threatens – but does not fire. It is as if he needs someone to absorb all his frustrations and insecurities and anxieties, and to take the blame for the Arsonist's failures to make his dreams into reality. If he eventually does fire that person, somebody else will soon take his place as the "villain on duty."

"Nothing is easier than fault-finding;
no talent, no self-denial, no brains, no character are
required to set up in the grumbling business."

ROBERT WEST

This is so consistently true that now, when I have an Arsonist as a client, I immediately look around for the "villain on duty." Who that person is will tell me a lot about the dynamics of the system.

On the other hand, Arsonists are easily swayed by people who admire or *appear* to admire them. A current client of mine has some employees who are not performing very well, but he doesn't fire them because they make him feel good. They listen, they look him in the eye, they're excited by his ideas.

If he fires or forces someone into resigning, it is predictable who will be eased out. You know who usually gets it? The (**A**)s. The (**A**) is, after all, constantly saying "no." He's the one who's slowing everything down. So he'll fire the (**A**)-type and bring in someone new.

The Arsonist's typical complaint about his staff is, "Nobody understands me." No one is following the priorities, he feels he's surrounded by idiots, and if they disagree with him in a meeting, that confirms they're idiots.

Whom does the (- - **E** -) like and appreciate? Predictably, his most recent hires. They are put on a pedestal – "Look at him! Look how good he is!" He walks on water – for a while. But it's temporary: soon enough that pedestal will be pulled unceremoniously from under them, and they will be thrown on the trash heap like all the rest before them, while the Arsonist starts looking around for the new savior of the day.

"Treat people as equals and the first thing you know they believe they are."

It is very difficult to consult to an Arsonist CEO. He'll admire you, he'll have no end of good words to say about you – until he meets the next genius and becomes infatuated. It might be someone he's met on a plane or at a meeting. It doesn't matter; from that point on, you'll find yourself abused and put down... but not fired.

Why not? (- - **E** -)s dislike firing people. They prefer to get a hatchet man to do the firing or, more often, they'll make your life so miserable that you'll eventually resign. They demean you, put you down, criticize you in public, humiliate you. But they don't usually fire, because they love applause and cannot stand the hard feelings that come with firing people. The Arsonist *gives* bad vibrations, but he cannot *take* them from others.

Subordinates

An Arsonist likes to hire (**I**)s, who will always agree with him. But (**I**)s are not good at (**P**)roducing, so when an Arsonist gives an (**I**) a task, nothing much will happen. The Arsonist very soon becomes frustrated, and complains bitterly: "It's difficult to soar like an eagle when you're surrounded by turkeys."

Subordinates avoid both the Arsonist and the Bureaucrat, but for opposite reasons. The Bureaucrat's subordinates avoid him because he is constantly telling them what they should *not* do. The Arsonist's subordinates avoid him because he is always assigning additional tasks, forgetting about the tasks he assigned earlier, which already fully occupy their time.

Managing Change

The Arsonist loves conflict. He often introduces it himself, using it to prod the organization into frantic activity. For the same reason, he loves change.

The job of a top manager is to identify for the organization the threats and opportunities inherent in the changing environment; and try to exploit the opportunities while providing protection against the threats. None of the mismanagement styles presented thus far does this. The Lone Ranger, the Bureaucrat, and the Arsonist all plan inadequately.

For the Arsonist, planning does not mean committing the organization to a course of action. To this type of mismanager, planning means presenting a long list of wishes. Whereas the Lone Ranger rarely takes the time to plan at all, and the Bureaucrat interprets planning to mean "forecasting" and derives next year's budget by adding some percentage to last year's results, the Arsonist may not even *have* a budget, and if he does it is usually unrealistic or out of date because it is constantly changing. Although he may not be sure which goals were actually achieved last year, he expects "quite a change" in the year to come. He also frequently exaggerates his goals and expectations in order to set fires under his subordinates' feet.

Tendency to Self-Destruct

The Arsonist is usually so preoccupied with opportunities that he sees few if any threats. He can endanger an organization by recklessly trying to exploit too many opportunities at once and spreading himself and his organization too thin. (- - **E** -)s can throw away an organization's profits by investing in a few half-baked ideas. As a Yugoslav proverb says, "What he builds during the day, he burns at night."

"For the creative mind, there is no right or wrong.
Every action is an experiment,
and every experiment yields its fruit in knowledge."

HAGBARD CELINE

Priorities

An Arsonist can get hung up on something that is minor as if it were something major. Conversely, he might ignore a major subject as if it were minor. An Arsonist would disagree with this statement, however: He believes that if people don't understand him and don't share his vision of the future, they are not fit to judge what is major and what is minor. And who knows; maybe he's right. (**E**)s march to their own drummer, on their own road, to their own destination. How can we judge?

Best Is the Enemy of Better

An (- - **E** -) assumes that change is always for better. I am an (**E**)-type, and when I write my books I am always revising and revising and revising. In the days before computers, I used to give my handwritten revisions to my secretary to retype. She would take my notes from my hand, look at me and ask, "Is it better, or is it just different?" She was extremely perceptive: (- - **E** -)s *do* tend to believe that if it's different, it's better. But that isn't necessarily the case. Best is the enemy of better. Because they aim for the best, constantly changing things in the belief that they are improving them, they never achieve finalization of their plans or an effective, efficient implementation.

Monopolization

One might expect to find creativity throughout an organization managed by an Arsonist, but the opposite is usually true. The Arsonist monopolizes the organization's creativity. He regards any other (**E**)ntrepreneurs as competitors and tries to neutralize or destroy them, as if "there is only one cock in the chicken coop."

Thus, an organization managed by an Arsonist is not a creative, flexible structure but a slave ship. The Arsonist sets the course, changes direction, ignores the suffering of his subordinates, and takes all the credit for successes.

CONCLUSION

Like the Lone Ranger and the Bureaucrat, the Arsonist bequeaths a mismanaged organization to his successor.

In the case of the (**P** - - -), no subordinates have been trained to take over. The (- **A** - -)'s subordinates are not creative and are afraid to take risks.

When the (- - **E** -) leaves, the organization is in chaos and its people are exhausted. They're desperate for peace and quiet, for stability, and they are convinced that anyone would be better than the Arsonist. As a result, they usually ask for and eventually get stuck with a Bureaucrat.

SUMMARY: CHARACTERISTICS OF THE ARSONIST STYLE

Behavior

Exclusive role: Innovator, (**E**)ntrepreneur.
He arrives at and leaves work: Randomly.
How he excels: Getting ideas and initiating new projects.
Predominant behavior: Creates new projects; questions everything; comes with his own agenda, disregarding the existing agenda.
Most distinctive personality traits: Enthusiastic, stimulating, charismatic, creative, and exciting. Wants the spotlight; charming to outsiders

(those he does not know); tough with insiders; criticizes people in public; looks for the hole in the donut instead of the donut; "Bugs Bunny syndrome" – full speed ahead, in neutral; seldom right but never in doubt; personalizes problems.

If he has free time: He will create a new project or crisis for the organization.

Appraises himself by: The existence of a beehive atmosphere; the appearance of productivity, usually manifested in crisis.

Communication

Offering feedback: Offers only negative feedback, and often. Will criticize in public. If you don't accept his criticism, he escalates the criticism. No one is good enough.

Focus and type of information he cherishes: Information on opportunities and threats.

Decision-Making

Technique: Temporary, no permanent commitments; proactive decisions, but no follow-up. To get things done, goes directly to those who can get it done instead of following established procedures. Negative decision reinforcement.

Implementing

Attitude toward systematic management: Avoids and abhors it; does not want to commit himself to anything.

Evaluating progress: Impatient: whatever progress has been made, it isn't enough.

Team-Building

Attitude toward conflict: Uses it to prod subordinates to frantic activity; frequently introduces it himself.

Attitude toward (P) type: Qualified approval.

Attitude toward (A) type: Abhors.

Attitude toward other (E) types: Resents.

Attitude toward (I) type: Likes.

Attitude toward Deadwood (- - - -): Ignores.

Typical complaints: "Things don't get done around here"; "They carry out the wrong priorities"; "They don't understand what I want, said, or meant to say."

Working together: Brushes off problems or solutions that other people have invested time and energy into; ideas aren't any good unless they're his ideas; and he insists on the right to change his decisions frequently.

Subordinates

He prefers to hire: A claque; admirers who accept his latest ideas enthusiastically and appear to understand them promptly.

Subordinates arrive and leave: Arrive before him and leave after him; are expected to be available at all hours.

Frequency and advance notice of staff meetings: Frequent and impromptu.

Staff meeting attendance: Required.

Staff meeting agenda: His latest idea is the first item; the rest is stream of consciousness.

Who talks at staff meetings: One-to-many, top-down; no questions asked; no details analyzed.

Subordinates are promoted: If they seem to follow directions enthusiastically and if they seem to work very hard at his assignments.

What subordinates get praised for: The appearance of hard work.

Subordinates do not inform him about: Why some of his project suggestions are bad ideas.

Dysfunctional behavior of subordinates: Producing excuses for lack of performance.

Managing Change

Focus of attention: What is new that is being done and how it might be done otherwise. His focus is a moving target.

Focus on issues: Sees threats as opportunities.

Training practices: Acceptable if they don't take time away from his latest pet project.

Attitude toward change: Thrives on it and loves it if he introduces it; resists it when generated by others.

Focus of creativity: Monopolized by him.

NOTES

1. For a definition of (E)ntrepreneurship, see Schumpeter, Joseph: *Business Cycles* (New York: McGraw Hill, 1939), pp. 102-9; and Drucker, Peter F.: *Management: Tasks, Responsibilities, Practices* (New York: Harper & Row, 1973), Chapter 10.

2. Adizes, Ichak: *How to Solve the Mismanagement Crisis* (Santa Monica, Calif.: Adizes Institute, Inc., 1979).

3. Fieve, Ronald R.: Moodswing: *Dr. Fieve on Depression* (New York: William Morrow and Co., 1989).

4. Maccoby, M.: "Narcissistic Leaders: The Incredible Pros, the Inevitable Cons," *Harvard Business Review* (January 1, 2001)

5. Lear, F.: *The Second Seduction* (New York: Alfred A. Knopf, 1992).

6. Rothchild, J.: *Going for broke: How Robert Campeau Bankrupted the Retail Iindustry, Jolted the Junk Bond Market and Brought the Booming Eighties to a Crashing Halt* (New York: Simon & Schuster, 1991).

7. Tillson, T.: "The CEO's disease," *Canadian Business*, 69 (3), (March 1996), pp. 26-30.

8. Strouse, J.: Morgan, *American Financier* (New York: Random House, 1999).

9. Bruck, C.: "The world of business," *The New Yorker*, 67 (3), (March 11, 1991), p. 40.

10. Tillson, T.: "The CEO's disease," op cit.

Chapter 5

The (I)ntegrator (pae**I**)

vs. the SuperFollower (- - - **I**)

Organizations are groups of people, and each of those people has needs, desires, and concerns. Members of an organization must be brought together; united around a central goal; and supported and nurtured in a culture of mutual trust and respect – in other words, they must be (**I**)ntegrated. (**I**)ntegrating an organization minimizes the waste of time and money and the internal politics that proliferate without it. It is a role that makes the company efficient in the long run, because when there is true teamwork, no one is indispensable and the organization can survive and even thrive despite the loss of any particular individual.

Management is continually faced with conflicting demands from outside the organization. In addition, friction arises *within* the organization because of differences in the styles, perspectives, and interests of the different people who comprise the organization. The (**I**) role is required to make such conflicts not only bearable but useful.[1]

GETTING RELIGION

Let's imagine a scenario. What would happen if your organization were managed by an executive who is an outstanding (**P**), (**A**), and (**E**)? This person is a knowledgeable, achievement-oriented, task-oriented, effective, no-nonsense (**P**)roducer; also an outstanding (**A**)d-ministrator – everything is efficient, correctly done at the right time – running a tight ship. The organization is effective and efficient. In addition, he is an outstanding (**E**)ntrepreneur – constantly proacting and improving so that the organization – can continue to adapt and adjust to its changing environment.

Now, what happens to this organization when this manager dies?

The organization also dies.

Why?

Because the (**P**), (**A**), and (**E**) roles are necessary, but they are not sufficient if the organization is to be effective and *efficient in the long run.*

Organizations should be managed so that they can survive for thousands of years. Look at the Catholic Church, for example. It has existed for two thousand years and it could go for another two thousand. Why? Because it has a set of values that each individual in the organization can understand and identify with. It is an organized religion – and like any organization, it needs the (**I**)ntegration role to be performed in order to build the organizational culture to which people adhere. (At the beginning of the 21st century, this (I)ntegration is threatened by a break in trust and respect, because of the sexual practices of some religious leaders.)

What is the biggest and most important asset a company can have? It isn't money; if there is a market, money will be glad to make itself available. It's not a market either. If you have the technology, you can find a market. Nor is it technology, because if there is money you can buy the technology.

Then what is it? It is a management that has the time to find the market, the money, and the technology and put them optimally together. For that, management needs time and energy. If the organization culture is ridden with disrespect and mistrust, most of the energy is wasted internally instead of on matching money to technology to markets. Thus, a culture of mutual trust and respect is the greatest asset a company can have. Even the best people cannot perform in a bad culture.

What you do as a company eventually can be copied, no matter how much protection you put into your intellectual property.

What you are is much more difficult to copy. It is easy to copy what Starbucks does. But try copying its organizational culture and you might find it to be impossible. And that culture might very well be the source of that organization's competitive edge.

Culture is the asset that is most difficult to build and the easiest to lose. Thus, all you growing companies: Beware! Do not outpace yourself. Do not grow so fast that you risk losing the culture that built you up in the first place.

As you can see, the role of (**I**)ntegration is extremely important. It is the role that builds the most important asset an organization can have.

The (**I**)ntegrator sees to it that we are working as a team and not as individuals. If the role of (**I**)ntegration is performed well, the team will be able to achieve or support any task that happens to be missing or deficient and necessary for its goal. It is important, therefore, that management have the ability to sense people's aspirations and needs, to recognize them and therefore be able to (**I**)ntegrate them.[2] Thus, a management style that leans toward the (**I**)ntegration role – someone who can help develop agreements and group support for ideas and their implementation – is crucial to a good management team.

The (**I**)ntegrator is concerned with smoothing the workings of the system from a people point of view. He is able to listen to people and to (**I**)ntegrate their ideas with other ideas.

(**I**)ntegration turns individual (**E**)ntrepreneurship into group (**E**)ntrepreneurship. An (**I**)ntegrator helps generate a decision that will be supported by those who will implement or be affected by that decision.

"The only way to have a friend is to be one."

RALPH WALDO EMERSON

(**I**)ntegration builds a climate, a system of ethics and behavior, that encourages everyone to work together so that no one is indispensable. To **(I)**ntegrate means to change the consciousness of the organization from mechanistic to organic.

Mechanistic means: "I care only for my own interests; you care only for yours." Look at a chair. If one of the legs breaks, does the other leg care about it? Why doesn't the healthy leg move to create a tripod so that the functionality of the chair – to enable sitting – continues? The reason it will not happen is that there is no internal sense of interdependency between the parts that constitute a chair. It is a mechanistic interdependency.

Now look at your hand. If one finger breaks, your whole body feels it. There is empathy. And not only that: When one finger breaks, the other four fingers on that hand will try to back it up, to compensate for the loss. That is organic interdependency. There is cooperation. It's synergetic instead of being individualistic, independent, and frequently adversarial.

(I)ntegration is what you should be doing in your family when the kids are fighting. You should not always give them a solution. You should say, "Hey, you are brothers or sisters, you're supposed to be helping each other. I'm not going to be here forever to solve your problems. You have to do it yourself." A family is more than a group of people, just as a hand is more than five fingers. There is interdependency. **(I)**ntegration involves making the team continue to function even if something happens to any individual member of the team.

Look at a sports team. If you take a team of stars, each from a different team, and put them together to play against an above average team with no stars but long experience in playing together as a team. Who might win the first game? The average team. Why? Because the star team has not yet developed its team consciousness. The team members cannot yet predict: "If he does *that*, I can back him up by doing *this*." That sense of cooperating to reach a common goal is what we mean by teamwork.

Interrelating is the ultimate purpose of our existence. There is nothing in this world that doesn't exist to serve something else by functionally interrelating to it. If it serves only itself, then it is a cancer, and serves death.

The pen I write with is useless if it does not leave a mark on paper. Breathing has no meaning unless the oxygen feeds my body. Nothing in itself is functional. The ability of anything to function must be measured and evaluated by how it serves its clients. The final purpose of existence of any system is (**I**)ntegration, the (**I**) role. In fact, managers with the ability to perform that role have the potential to go beyond good management and become leaders.

"Getting together is a beginning.
Staying together is progress.
Working together is success."

HENRY FORD I

If a manager does not (**I**)ntegrate, does not nourish group (**E**)ntrepreneurship, then in extreme cases the group will be unable to initiate action or determine goals in his absence. Companies that rely on any one individual for continuous success in their operations inevitably will face a crisis if that individual leaves or dies. Even organizations that have been managed by a (**PAE-**) have found themselves in trouble if that manager leaves before a team feeling – an *esprit de corps* around an effective course of action – has been developed. Since an organization's life span is longer than the life of any individual, effective long-range continuity depends on building a team of people who understand, trust, and respect each other, and who complement each other's abilities. (**I**)ntegration creates that effect.

When there is no (**I**)ntegration taking place, no one is focused on the company's culture of interdependence. Instead, everybody is looking out for their own interests, often at the expense of the company. The stockholders are trying to milk the company. Management is trying to get maximum rewards for itself. Labor is trying to get the best salaries and the best security at work. Among such competing interests, it's possible to arrive at a working consensus in which everyone is working hard, but the company is actually going bankrupt.

When I find a situation like this in the organizations I coach, I often dramatize the dilemma by bringing an empty chair to the table. I place the company name on the front of the chair, and ask, "If someone were sitting in that chair, what would he say? What does *this company* want?" When I let the participants play out that scenario, I hear voices that have previously been silent. In this exercise, I am playing the (I)ntegrating role.

THE (I)NTEGRATOR (pael)

There are two types of (I)ntegration – passive and active – and three directions: Upward, lateral, and downward.

A passive (I)ntegrator will (I)ntegrate himself into a group of people. An active (I)ntegrator can (I)ntegrate a group of people among themselves. Because in management, (I)ntegration must be active, we will concern ourselves here only with active (I)ntegration.

Upward (I)ntegration is the ability to (I)ntegrate people who are higher in status, authority, rank, and so on. Lateral (I)ntegration is the ability to (I)ntegrate peers into a cohesive group. Downward (I)ntegration provides leadership by establishing cohesion among subordinates.

A very effective upward (I)ntegrator may function poorly as a downward (I)ntegrator – tending to be arrogant with subordinates. In fact, it is unusual for a person to be an excellent (I)ntegrator in all directions.[5]

Let's talk about the characteristics that a good (I)ntegrator brings to the organization.

Perhaps surprisingly, (I)ntegration is the most creative of all the roles, since decisions have to be made from a more diffused and less structured database. (I)ntegrating is even less programmable than (E)ntrepreneuring, because (E)ntrepreneuring does not necessarily deal with people, whereas (I)ntegrating involves uniting individuals with diverse interests and strengths behind a group decision. Thus, a great deal more creativity is required to (**I**)ntegrate or unite a group of (**E**)ntrepreneurs than to merely make an (**E**)ntrepreneurial contribution.

In (**I**)ntegrating (**E**)ntrepreneurs, one has the additional burden of (**I**)ntegrating their individual creativities into a cohesive unity – to forge group risk-taking out of individual risk-taking, to fuse an *individual* sense of responsibility into a *group* sense of responsibility.

(**I**)ntegration is accomplished by clarifying issues, by finding the common threads of agreement – in deep rather than superficial issues – and by analyzing contrasting values, assumptions, and expectations.

A successful (**I**)ntegrator also must make himself dispensable. His subordinates must be trained to be capable of replacing him. Ideally, in a cohesive group almost any member can initiate action, (**A**)dminister programs, and (**P**)roduce results. To take a military example, if any soldier in a squad can take the squad leader's place and be accepted by the squad when the leader is killed, this demonstrates that the leader was a good (**I**)ntegrator. If the squad scatters when the leader is killed, this shows that the (**I**)ntegration of the unit was insufficient, though the leader may have been a competent commander in other respects.

The (**I**)ntegrator not only provides for future organizational continuity, but also enables the organization to function smoothly in the present.

The (**I**)ntegrator is sensitive to others (i.e., empathetic), and he is capable of deductive thinking (i.e., able to infer what people really *want* to say from what they *do* say). He has few ego problems of his own, which enables him to hear and respond to other people's expectations, problems, and needs rather than his own.

The late Juscelino Kubitschek, former president of Brazil and founder of Brasilia, was very (**I**)-oriented. I was told that when asked whether he was for or against a certain political program, he replied: "I am neither for nor against it: I am above it."

THE (I) ROLE IN LEADERSHIP

The (**I**) role is unique because it is the one role that must be present in order for leadership to occur.

Along with their other abilities, all leaders must motivate, inspire, and (**I**)ntegrate. Thus, there are several styles of leaders: (**PaeI**), whom I call the Shepherd; (**pAeI**), the Participative Administrator; (**paEI**), the Statesman; (**PaeI**), the Benevolent Prince; and (**PaEI**), the Change Leader.

Managers can be strong in two or even three roles–(**PAei**), (**PaEi**), (**pAEi**), (**PAEi**) – but unless one of them is (**I**)ntegrating, they will not be leaders. For leadership to occur, the (**I**) role must enhance whatever other roles a manager excels at performing. And of course, none of them can be blanks.

THE SUPERFOLLOWER (- - - I)

How would a manager function if he were deficient in the areas of (**P**)roducing, (**A**)dministrating, and (**E**)ntrepreneuring and was only capable of (**I**)ntegrating?

This manager's code would look like this: (- - - **I**). What is he mostly concerned about? He's concerned about who. He doesn't care what we agree about, nor how we agree about it, nor why we agree. The important thing is: "Do we agree?" I call him the SuperFollower.

Behavior

What are the characteristics that typify a SuperFollower?

He's not a leader. He's the one who asks, "Where would you like to go? Let me lead you there."

An (- - - **I**) accommodates endlessly. He wants everything to run smoothly. So, like an (- **A**- -) who gets stuck in the deliberation phase of decision-making, an (- - - **I**) gets stuck in the accommodations phase. He tries to find out what plan will be acceptable to the largest number of powerful people and then tries to unite them behind that plan. That is, he does not really lead – he follows. He merely unifies people, regardless of the cause. That's why I call him a SuperFollower.

The SuperFollower is like a fish monitoring the undercurrent, always seeking the right tide to carry himself forward. He's a cheap politician, always listening to what is going on, trying to sense the undercurrent: "What do these people want? Let me lead them there."

"Stand for something, lest you fall for anything."

AMERICAN EXPRESSION

This is precisely the difference between a politician and a statesman: The statesman worries about the next generation, while the politician worries about the next election. The SuperFollower is not concerned about the next generation; he's concerned about the next election: "Do we agree?" He might be running a very happy disaster. He negotiates an *appearance* of agreement rather than resolving the deep-seated issues that cause conflict. "We have a consensus," he announces triumphantly – but the company's going broke.

As an example, in the 1990s I was a go-between in negotiations between the Greek and the Macedonian prime ministers. Greece was demanding that Macedonia change its name, out of concern that the name might encourage extreme nationalism and cause turbulence in the large Macedonian population of northern Greece. To further pressure the Macedonians, the Greek government placed an economic embargo on Macedonia, whom they called FYROM (Former Yugoslav Republic of Macedonia.) That country was now landlocked, surrounded by enemies in all directions. Removing the Greek embargo was of vital importance.

I convinced the Greeks to remove the embargo if Macedonia would agree to change its name to New (*Nova*) Macedonia. But the Macedonian premier said, "No way." Why? "Because if I do that, I'm going to lose in the election and there'll be riots in the streets."

This was a typical SuperFollower response. He was going for the vote, worrying about the polls. But a true statesman is less self-interested than that. He would fight for the company (or the country)

– and if he loses the election, so be it. Take Shimon Peres of Israel. He repeatedly lost in elections. He had the image of being a loser. Why? He was not following the polls. He was following his vision, which he tried to transmit and convince the voters to follow. He was a great statesman and poor politician.

A politician watches his feet to avoid stumbling–while a states-man (**paEI**) watches the horizon and frequently stumbles, politically. Winston Churchill, who lost elections more than once but stuck to his vision nevertheless, was an example of a statesman.

The SuperFollower likes to train, but most of his training is focused on interpersonal relations. He wants to know who thinks what about whom, and he wants everyone to agree on everything. He welcomes any training – *if* it improves his ability to understand human nature or contributes to the appearance of unity.

If the SuperFollower has free time, he spends it socializing, listening to complaints or agreements, and then amplifying and ac-centuating them with his support.

Like the other three types, the SuperFollower wants control – but in his case it's a bizarre kind of control that's unique to this type. An (- - - I) wants to control by having everybody agree. He won't tolerate political deviations. In this way, he can be as suffocating as a Bureaucrat–perhaps worse. The SuperFollower's rules are unwritten, but everyone has to follow them. The values of the system are imposed on everyone, and disagreement is the same as betrayal.

COMMUNICATION

The SuperFollower doesn't tell you what he thinks; he asks you what you think. He's always trying to find out which way the wind is blow-ing–where the agreement is, where the resistance is, where the weak-est spot of resistance is – so that he can locate the political common ground.

So he's noncommittal. He might say something like, "I have an idea, but I'm not so sure I agree with it," or "I suggest we declare dividends, but I don't feel too strongly about it."

"I cannot give you the formula for success,
but I can give you the formula for failure:
Try to please everybody all the time."

HERBERT BAYARD SWOPE

What is he doing? He's sending up trial balloons to see which way the wind is blowing. If you tell him something is a bad idea, he'll agree: "I *knew* it. I thought so too."

It's difficult to get a SuperFollower to commit to a point of view. In Mexico, they call this type of manager "the soapy fish," because you just can't catch him. He always has some way to slip away; he always wiggles out of your hands. His typical complaint is: "You didn't understand what I really wanted to say." You can't corner him. He's a political animal; he can read the power base faster than anybody else. That's how he remains in power for a long time: he figures out which side is winning and adapts himself to that side.

On the one hand, this slipperiness gives him a lot of power, because people are always worrying, "What is *he* thinking?" I had an executive who was a big (- - - **I**). Whenever anyone went to tell him about a problem, he would write it down in a big notebook. He'd listen. He'd ask questions, he'd research the subject. Then you'd ask him, "What do you think?" and he'd say, "Let me think about it." But you'd never hear back from him.

So people don't know where the SuperFollower stands; they never know what he's going to do. At the same time, he's accumulated an enormous amount of information from everything people tell him, and the more information he has, the more power he has. People don't dare challenge him because of his position and because they don't know what he thinks.

DECISION-MAKING

The Lone Ranger usually makes very quick, practical decisions, based on technical knowledge, and then he gets right out there and implements them. The Bureaucrat likes decisions to be in writing so that he can assign accountability and penalties for any rule violations. This is in direct contrast to the approach of the Arsonist, who hates to have decisions in writing because he wants the process to remain as fluid as possible.

The SuperFollower, on the other hand, tends to avoid making his own decisions altogether, as long as he can. When decisions must be made, he would rather work toward a consensus than make a decision by himself.

"If you want to get along, go along."

SAM RAYBURN

The exclusive (- - - **I**) has no ideas of his own that he would like to implement—no (**E**); no tangible results that he wants to achieve—no (**P**). Like the Bureaucrat, who does not care what he (**P**)roduces so long as it is implemented efficiently, the SuperFollower shows little concern about what he (**I**)ntegrates. All he wants is the appearance of consensus, a "united front." But unlike an (- **A** - -), he is indifferent to any particular system, as long as agreement is achieved or is seen to be achieved.

Gerald Bell called this style of manager "The Pleaser."[3] The Pleaser wants very much to be liked and works hard at it. He dislikes conflict and has a strong need for acceptance. He is group-reliant rather than self-reliant; therefore, he prefers not to make decisions alone.

One reason he could never be a true leader is because he cannot take the heat.

"If you can't take the heat, get out of the kitchen."

HARRY TRUMAN

Because of his need to please, he does not have strong convictions; thus his mind can be changed quickly and easily. He sways with popular opinions. Bell quotes a Pleaser as saying during a board meeting, "I really think we should seek new financing through a stock issue." As he was speaking, other directors began shaking their heads in disagreement. Almost without pausing, the Pleaser continued, "but I don't feel strongly about this point."

IMPLEMENTING

During implementation, an (- - - I) tends to have doubts and worries about the decision, especially if there is no clear consensus about it. He wastes a lot of time explaining the decision, even apologizing for it. The more he explains and apologizes, the more power he loses.

Sometimes a SuperFollower will postpone and postpone a decision until there's a consensus, but his procrastination can have a high price. While he waits, opportunities disappear.

"Even if you're on the right track,
you'll get run over if you just sit there."

WILL ROGERS

The (- - - I) has trouble being satisfied with what I call a workable consensus, which means it may not be perfect but it has enough support that it can be effectively implemented. If someone disagrees, tough luck, because we need to move on. It's a practical strategy – a very (P)-strategy, if you will. But the SuperFollower does not grasp that there is value in making *timely* decisions – that it is better to have a somewhat disputable decision implemented on time, than a universally supported decision that is implemented too late.

Another concept the SuperFollower doesn't understand is that once people agree, that does not necessarily mean they are actually going to follow through and implement the decision.

Some (- - - I)s seem to think, "If we agreed on it, my task is finished." They do not realize that the so-called agreement might be only the *appearance* of an agreement. Those who work with a Super-Follower know very well what strategy will get them off the hook: the appearance of consensus. This is a real threat to implementation, because the appearance of consensus is *not* consensus, and if the group doesn't own a decision, nothing will happen.

TEAM-BUILDING

At meetings, a SuperFollower can easily be identified. Consider a hypothetical meeting at which the four different types of mismanagers – the Lone Ranger, Bureaucrat, Arsonist, and SuperFollower – are present.

Who is doing most of the talking? The Arsonist. The Bureaucrat is busy disagreeing with something or other or taking notes. The Lone Ranger is restless, not paying attention, running out every few minutes to make a call, or flipping through his correspondence at the conference table while the others argue.

The SuperFollower is listening attentively. Who is saying what? What did they *really* mean to say? What is *not* being said? Where does the power lie? Which way is the decision likely to go?

He is trying to identify each participant's motives and the basis of any conflict. He is looking for the secret agendas. He rarely presents viable new alternatives, but if he does, he doesn't care how many times he changes his suggestions as long as an increasing number of people find them acceptable.

If you want to know what happened in a meeting, don't ask an Arsonist. He heard very little of it; he was either busy talking or listening to his own ideas. Don't ask the Bureaucrat, either; he was busy taking notes in such detail that he missed the point of the discussion. And definitely don't ask the Lone Ranger. He heard nothing! Either he was too busy signing papers, or else he arrived late and left early.

Ask an (**I**). He knows who said what, why he said it; who did not say anything and why not and even what he *would* have said if the circumstances had been different.

If the SuperFollower is chairing the meeting and a consensus cannot be achieved, he will probably postpone making a decision by establishing a subcommittee to study the problem further, until the political winds change direction and a consensus can be reached.

This (- - - **I**) type falls into the low-task, high social range (0.9) of Blake and Mouton's managerial grid,[4] a model they formulated to describe managerial behavior.

Blake and Mouton's grid has two axes: "Task" and "orientation to people." According to their model, the SuperFollower is extremely sensitive and responsive to what others think. He cannot tolerate rejection, so in order to avoid it, he avoids rejecting others. He rarely expresses preferences of his own, usually accepting the opinions, attitudes, and ideas of those around him. "As a result," say Blake and Mouton, "when convictions are expressed, they are more likely to be reflections of what his boss, his peers, or his subordinates think and want, as opposed to his own convictions and desires. He is rarely in an initiating role in issues that call for exerting positive leadership."[5]

There are two sides to every question
and if you want to be popular – you take both.

Source unknown

If a power struggle develops among members of the organization, the SuperFollower is preternaturally gifted at divining which side will win. Then he will lend himself to that side, even appearing to lead it.

His method of arriving at unity is to keep working for compromise among the various parties involved. He is unlikely to support controversial alternatives – especially if they require concessions from the dominant group.

On the other hand, and almost paradoxically, the SuperFollower thrives on power struggles – providing he can control them. Because he generally advocates the dominant, short-term acceptable option rather than working to achieve a long-term, uplifting, and unifying alternative, his solutions never last, ensuring that people will continually be turning against each other.

If the SuperFollower is the leader of an organization, it can quickly become dysfunctional because he usually stops short of really uniting people, settling for the illusion of unity. For unity, a deep recognition of common goals is necessary, and all (**P**), (**A**), (**E**), *and* (**I**) roles need to be acknowledged. Without (**E**) to provide a long-term unifying vision, for instance, the group can never become (**I**)ntegrated in the long run, much less effective or efficient. Because of this, power struggles can be fatal under the SuperFollower.

On the lower level of the organizational hierarchy, this behavior is dysfunctional in a different way. People eventually come to believe the SuperFollower has nothing to say, and they learn to ignore him. Although initially the SuperFollower accumulates power by gathering information and playing it close to the vest, depending on his position in the hierarchy, he might actually be losing power.

In a team context, the SuperFollower will never initiate conflict. An (- - **E** -) sows conflict. An (- - **E** -) will tell Jack why Bill is terrible and tell Bill why Ann is terrible and tell Ann why Jack is terrible. A (**P**- - -) will ignore conflict; there is too much to do. An (- **A** - -) will attempt to legislate conflict out of existence.

The SuperFollower will become involved in a dispute only if it will increase his stature and power. In fact, he interprets the tensions that accompany conflict as a rejection of himself. An (- - - **I**) makes sure he is in control by being instrumental in the resolution of the conflict. If this is impossible, if he cannot resolve the conflict, he will simply not get involved. He will not throw himself into the crossfire, potentially risking his position and power in order to resolve a conflict. Thus, he is perfectly capable of watching Rome burn without lifting a hose to help.

He works to relieve tensions, to achieve unity, temporarily if necessary, no matter what the long-term costs may be. This quality was also observed by Blake and Mouton, who suggest that such a person rarely generates conflict but that when conflict appears, either between himself and others or between others, he tries to soothe bad feelings. When tensions between people arise, the SuperFollower attempts to reduce them.

But this desire to resolve conflicts can be destructive rather than helpful in the long run, if future interests are not represented in the process of conflict resolution. The SuperFollower is less interested in these than in the interests of his immediate constituency.

MANAGING STAFF

If the Lone Ranger's subordinates are gofers, those of the Bureaucrat yes-yes people, and the Arsonist's are a claque, then how would one characterize the followers of the SuperFollower? They are informers, or oilers. What do they spend their time on? "What's going on?" "Who said what?" "What does it mean?" "Where is the power base?"

The SuperFollower hires people like himself, who are politically intuitive; they have a good nose for how the political power base is moving. They are the first to identify it and to jump on the bandwagon.

Their main jobs are to keep the boss up-to-date and keep everybody happy. It is their duty to feed the boss the latest office "news"; no gossip is too insignificant to relate, as long as it adds to his trove of information about people, positions, attitudes, and opinions within the company.

But the SuperFollower's subordinates know better than to inform him about real, deep conflicts. They know he is too shallow to be capable of handling situations where he actually has to take a stand; he is too wishy-washy.

In his presence, the (- - - I)'s subordinates appear peaceful and accepting, remembering that their boss prefers people whom other people like. In order to be promoted by the SuperFollower, they know they must be accepted by others. This often requires them to hide their true feelings from him, which can easily lead to their feeling manipulated and emotionally exploited.

Subordinates react to this type of management with everything from enthusiasm to apathy or rebellion, depending on whether they've learned how to get what they want from the SuperFollower and the organization itself. A rebellion can arise when the company is following a direction that a minority knows to be disastrous. Sometimes, either to attract attention or to "ease out" a colleague, the SuperFollower's subordinates will instigate rumors that unity is in danger.

MANAGING CHANGE

I was told about an executive at a high-tech company whose (- - - **I**) style had initially served the company well. He gave a lot of space to the tech people. He didn't compete with them, he always tried to find out what they thought, and then what others thought, and he never got involved in any of the political in-fighting or corporate ego trips that high-tech, creative types are prone to. Everyone was able to express himself, and this executive stayed neutral, while the company just grew bigger and bigger. His role was not to tell them what to do; his role was only to look at the boundaries of what not to do so that they did not grow too fast or in the wrong direction.

It was a perfect style for a high-tech company where egos are crucial for success – *until* the company had to reinvent itself. Because the industry had matured in its life cycle, this company needed a major re-engineering job. Technology no longer drove the industry; what was becoming more important to their clients was reliability, quality, cost, and better management of the supply chain. The company needed to change its strategies and direction.

This required that someone step into the intersection and begin redirecting traffic in a different direction. It required a (**P**) style: somebody who could go in, take the bull by the horns and say, "Stop! No more of *this*; now we're going to do *that*."

Well, this manager was not of that style. So increasingly he was being ignored, and because there was a vacuum where leadership should have been, more and more antagonism was being directed toward him, his performance, and his abilities, and the company suffered.

A painful change is like going on a diet: sometimes you need to do it or your excess weight will cause diabetes or a heart attack. What *must* be done is not necessarily what you *want* to be done. But the (- - - **I**) type refuses to acknowledge the necessity of pain; the adage "No pain, no gain" doesn't register with him.

A SuperFollower, being a politician, will not take the risk or undertake the fighting necessary to upset the short-term consensus in order to reach long-term goals. He is not a statesman, who is willing to risk conflict in the short run because he sees the necessity of change over the long run. Achieving a consensus that will benefit future generations means undertaking projects whose outcome is uncertain. This involves political risk, and the SuperFollower avoids taking such risks.

The (- - - **I**) will not attempt to lift himself above the organization's most pressing interests; he will not attempt to sway the direction the organization should take. He will not threaten an existing consensus. He does not like to confront subordinates. He will not absorb the aggression that is created when a course of action offends a particular group.

Instead, he tries to identify himself with a direction that is already acceptable to the organization. He is always asking, "What do we agree about?" Then, he will adopt the opinion of the more powerful group rather than coming up with his own suggestions.

What are the SuperFollower's goals? The goals of the Lone Ranger and the Bureaucrat are very short-term: The Lone Ranger just wants to get the job done, and the Bureaucrat wants to keep the system tight and intact. Long-range goals are more likely to be found in the activities of the Arsonist. However, the Arsonist's goals tend to be scattered.

The SuperFollower has no particular goal; or rather, the goal is whatever is most desired at a particular time by a consensus of his co-workers. His behavior could be compared to a school of fish that swims in the direction of the prevailing current. The "current," rather than a specific goal, determines his direction. This is, of course, a very limited attitude toward corporate goals, and as a result, short-range interest groups flourish under the SuperFollower.

What about planning?

A good manager responds to environmental opportunities and threats by formulating strategies. We know that the Lone Ranger is so busy working that he hardly ever even *sees* threats or opportunities. The Arsonist, on the other hand, is so preoccupied with potential opportunities that he fails to recognize immediate threats. For him, planning is mostly dreaming up ideas, exchanging views, and getting people excited. Planning consists of endlessly discussing what might be, as opposed to what is possible or practical. And the Bureaucrat sees planning as an excuse to establish more rules. For him, planning means scheduling, coordinating details, setting control points, and establishing report systems.

The SuperFollower uses planning as a means for exchanging views, as a consciousness-raising experience in which people express their individual aspirations and expectations, or as an occasion for identifying conflicts that he can subsequently resolve. He might say, "What is your vision? What are your scenarios of the future?" When conflicting aspirations and expectations are clarified, he seeks to (I)ntegrate them. Unfortunately, he can only (I)ntegrate them superficially, since he lacks the (E)-qualities that are needed to resolve deep-seated differences by providing a long-term unifying vision.

CONCLUSION

Over the long-term, management under a SuperFollower can be disastrous. The SuperFollower lacks purpose, direction, and courage. Without a unified, consistent, conscious long-term policy, the organization is hostage to the power structure shifts within it and will either change direction continually or become petrified. Either outcome is ineffective and inefficient in the long run, and often even in the short run.

When a SuperFollower leaves an organization, the superficial (**I**)ntegration he established will rapidly deteriorate. Middle-level managers are likely to start pulling in different directions, destabilizing the fragile unity of the organization and threatening to shake it apart. At that point, an (**A**)-type is often called in to resolve the problem. This solution can be traumatic, as it replaces the (**I**)ntegration of people, the development of appropriate compromises, with a rigid set of regulations to force order.

THE COMMON DENOMINATOR

For all their differences, the four managerial styles – (**P- - -**), (- **A- -**), (- - **E-**), and (- - - **I**) – have one trait in common: They are all inflexible stereotypes. The managers who exhibit these styles have unidimensional, one-track minds. They have only a limited perception of who they are and of what they are supposed to do in life.[6] They are not wellrounded individuals.

Like the (**P- - -**), who tries so hard to be effective that he ignores the (A) role, rendering his organization inefficient; like the (- **A - -**), who wants so badly to be efficient that he controls every little detail to the point of making the company ineffective; like the (- - **E -**), who is so focused on change that he creates paralyzing chaos; the exclusive (- - - **I**), by avoiding explicit conflict, creates a climate where implicit conflict abounds.

Inflexible, unidimensional behavior is one cause of mismanagement. But more important, inflexibility has negative effects on the individual and on his ability to function effectively and efficiently in the organization. Anyone who is inflexible, who exhibits an exclusive management style, is in danger of becoming a fanatic, a martyr, or a Deadwood. The Deadwood is described in the next chapter.

Summary: Characteristics of the SuperFollower

Behavior

Exclusive role: (**I**)ntegrator of people.

He arrives at and leaves work: Appropriately; as expected by everyone else.

Most distinctive personality traits: Smooth, sensitive, people-oriented, understanding, thankful for being introduced into the secrets of the organization. Good listener.

Focus of attention: The acceptability of what is done or might be done.

Appraises himself by: How central he is to the power play.

Typical complaint: "We do not get along as well as we should."

If he has free time: He will identify new conflicts (even imaginary ones) that only he can resolve; will spread rumors or collect information to the effect that such conflicts exist.

Communication

Predominant behavior: Compromising, (**I**)ntegrating people's ideas.

Focus and type of information he cherishes: Who stands where on what issues; will not share it.

Decision-Making

Technique: Will make decisions only when there is a group consensus.

Implementing

Attitude toward systematic management: Is suspicious of it because it might disturb the power structure he controls.

Team-Building

How he excels: Getting agreement, compromising.

Attitude toward conflict: Likes it if he can be instrumental in resolving it.

Attitude toward (P) type: Dismisses as stupid.

Attitude toward (A) type: Avoids; sees (A)'s as barriers to consensus-building.

Attitude toward (E) type: Plays up to because they usually dominate.

Attitude toward other (I) types: Suspicious of, if they do not work for him. Accepts and protects them if they work for him.

Attitude toward Deadwood (- - - -): Likes them a lot because they cause no trouble.

Managing Staff

He prefers to hire: Submissive people, people who get along with each other and with him.

Subordinates' style: Informers.

Subordinates arrive and leave: Appropriately; as expected; with him.

Frequency and advance notice of staff meetings: Regular, as expected.

Staff meeting attendance: Desired.

Staff meeting agenda: Freewheeling, whatever people want to talk about.

Who talks at staff meetings: Anyone and everyone, as long as they do not threaten his political dominance.

Subordinates are promoted: If they get along and are supportive and loyal to him politically.

What subordinates get praised for: Getting along.

Subordinates do not inform him about: Their true feelings if those feelings might destroy a consensus.

Dysfunctional behavior of subordinates: Create rumors to get attention.

Managing Change

Attitude toward change: Accepts it if it augments his role as a conflict resolver and does not impair unity.

Attitude toward planning: Will fight it if he considers it a threat to the pseudo-unity he's created, or if it will make him dispensable.

Focus of creativity: (I)ntegrated by him.

Training practices: Focused on interpersonal relations.

NOTES

1. On the role of Integration, see Lawrence, P.R., and J. W. Lorsch, "New Managerial Job: The (I)ntegrator," *Harvard Business Review*, 45 (November 1967), pp. 142-51.

2. The (I) component, as has been pointed out, is essential to good management at all levels, because the manager must work through others to achieve organizational goals. Where management has succeeded in (I)ntegrating the individual members of an organization into a group, we may expect greater identification with the organization, more job satisfaction, and better performance. The importance of interpersonal relationships for the success of organizations has been repeatedly demonstrated in the literature. Chris Argyris found that the worker's skill and pride in his work were directly related to his on-the-job friendships. See Argyris, "The Fusion of an Individual with the Organization," *American Sociological Review*, 19 (1954), pp. 14567; and "Personality vs. Organization," Organizational Dynamics, 3 (1974) no. 2, pp. 217.

   A similar association between level of competence and degree of (I)ntegration with the organization was reported by Peter M. Blau in a study of law enforcement agents. See Blau, "Patterns of Interaction among a Group of Officials in a Government Agency," *Human Relations*, 7 (1954), pp. 337-48.

3. Gerald Bell, *The Achievers* (Chapel Hill, N.C.: Preston Hill, 1973), Ch. 7.

4. Blake, Robert, and Jane Mouton: *The Managerial Grid* (Houston: Gulf Publishing, 1964), p. 75.

5. Ibid., p. 77.

6. I am grateful to Bob Tannenbaum of UCLA for having directed my attention to this common characteristic.

Chapter 6

Characteristics of Deadwood (----)

"Inevitably, when you do have that very fortunate circumstance of the man and the moment meeting, the situation begins to deteriorate because the moment changes; and the man is very reluctant to change. Sooner or later, the man becomes an anachronism because he no longer suits the situation. He cannot change that much, so he will not accept the fact that the moment has changed. He will denounce the world because it wouldn't freeze itself in his moment."

RALPH ABLON

Deadwood is apathetic. He waits to be told what to do. He might work hard, like the Lone Ranger, but the results are not there; he does not get involved with power intrigues, like the SuperFollower; he does not provide sparks, as does the Arsonist. If he has any good ideas or opinions, he keeps them to himself. Unlike the Bureaucrat, Deadwood cares about following the rules only insofar as doing so will help him survive until retirement.

His only goal is to keep intact the little world he has created. He knows that any change threatens his position. To maximize his chances for survival, he avoids change by avoiding new jobs or projects. He does not resist anything. Resisting will expose him and make him vulnerable. So he agrees to everything and takes action on nothing.

DUNAGIN'S PEOPLE - By Ralph Dunagin

"And I remind you that I have served you for two terms without causing any harm."

Deadwood is agreeable, friendly, and non-threatening. He is liked, much as a friendly old uncle is liked, but he is not respected. So people endure him and do not want to hurt him. In the meantime, the organization suffers.

In his free time, the Deadwood looks for successes that he can take credit for. He is usually out of the information network, but if he does get access to any information, he cherishes it and uses it at every conceivable opportunity, even when it's irrelevant – just to prove that he's still plugged in and kicking.

Gerald Bell, in his studies of management, has identified an analogous personality style, which he calls the Avoider.[1] The Avoider refrains from making decisions and gets others to choose the jobs and goals to be accomplished. If possible, the Avoider will limit himself to tasks that are easy to identify and accomplish.

Rangnekar's Rules for Decision Avoidance
Rule 1: If you can avoid a decision, do so.
Rule 2: If you can avoid a decision, don't delay it.
Rule 3: If you can get somebody else to avoid a
decision, don't avoid it yourself.
Rule 4: If you cannot get one person to avoid the
decision, appoint a committee.

THOMAS L. MARTIN, JR.

Bell's Avoider has a low tolerance for criticism or humiliation. Thus, he spends a lot of energy just trying to avoid trouble. An organization managed by an Avoider tends to shrink and lose touch with the outside world. Instead of adapting to situational demands, the Avoider ignores them. According to Bell, "Left under his direction, his department will slowly become invisible."[1]

But the situation can become even more serious than that. Deadwood can actually be fatal to an organization.

Four distinct characteristics mark Deadwood as distinct from any other mismanagement style:

No. 1: "Low Managerial Metabolism"

Deadwood very likely started out as one of the other four types of mismanagers, and he still evinces his former dominant personality traits. One can still see in him traces of the enthusiastic Arsonist or the meticulous Bureaucrat. But by the time he has become Deadwood, his No. 1 characteristic is a "low managerial metabolism."

He smokes or drinks a lot. He coughs, hums, and nods his head in agreement – "Uh huh"; "Oh yes, sure"; he confides to you how well he is doing, or how well he did in the past, or how well he will do, but nothing is happening. No energy. You sense that not much is to be expected from him. He is only going through the motions.

No. 2: Deadwood Has No Complaints

Each of the previous four types has a typical complaint: "The day is too short" (**P**); "It's not being done the way it should be done" (**A**); "The most urgent priorities are not being followed" (**E**); "They did not understand what I really wanted to say" (**I**).

Deadwood? If you ask him, "How is it going? Any problems?" "No, no! Everything is fine."

To be alive is to be always working on something. That is how you grow and develop. You're trying to resolve or improve something. If there are no problems, then there are no opportunities either.

But Deadwood thinks a complaint would reflect badly on him or perhaps result in changes he cannot handle. He might actually be asked to solve the problems he is complaining about. To avoid threats to his existence, he never complains. Everything is always going well; everything is fine. The company may be going bankrupt, but if you ask, "How are you doing?" he will always tell you, "Fine. Everything is fine." He has no ax to grind. It's very quiet. You never hear any griping from him or his department. To his supervisor, that may seem like a good thing.

No. 3: No Resistance to Change

Each of the other styles will resist change for one reason or another. If you go to the Lone Ranger and say, "This item needs to move from here to there," what will he say? "I have no time. When am I going to do it? I am too busy. I'm falling apart!"

"Now look," you might respond, "I did not say *you* should move it. I said: *It* needs to be moved." But the Lone Ranger identifies everything that needs to be done as *his* responsibility. And if he cannot do it, then nobody should do it. So everybody else is just sitting there, while he is frantically working. He is a bottleneck.

To get around the Lone Ranger, you have to tell him that there is a *crisis*. Then he will hear you. And tell him that if he cannot take care of it, then someone else must do it – because it is a *crisis*.

"Okay," he'll sigh. "Put it on my desk, and I will move it."

If you go to the Bureaucrat and say, "We need to move this item from here to there," he's going to yell "No!" before you even finish the sentence. Why? Because he can foresee all the side effects, the undesirable repercussions that could arise because we moved the item from one place to another. An (**A**) sees the cost of everything and the value of nothing. He will tell you there is no way to move this item – "*unless*" – and the "unless" will be so complicated that you will either give up the effort, or else do it without telling him about it.

To get around the Bureaucrat's resistance, you have to say, "This item in this location is violating a policy"– any prior decision will do. "It's breaking a rule." For the Bureaucrat, the "violation" legitimizes this task as a problem.

Next, you have to say, "The movement of the item from here to there has already been done ten times before, and here is the documentation. There is no risk, no problem." Or you can say, "I take full responsibility for this action." Then he will say, "All right. Let's move it." He will always give you resistance to change unless you convince him either that there is no risk or that someone else is taking the risk.

Now let us go to the Arsonist. "We would like to move this item from here to there." The Arsonist says, "What a great idea! A fantastic idea! But you know what? While you're moving this item from here to there, why don't you move this other item as well from there to here, and also take this third item and put it over here, and then drop that building down...."

"Wait a minute!" you'll protest. "All we wanted to do is move this item from here to there."

But once he's started, the Arsonist will want to change *every-thing*. He de facto resists change by insisting that if there is going to be change, it has to be his idea. And usually it is not one idea but a whole lot of ideas. Thus, the Arsonist is very dangerous. You go into his office asking for a solution to one problem, and you leave with ten new problems you have to solve.

I am an Arsonist myself. My secretary once gave me a T-shirt for my birthday; on the front it said "BIG (**E**)"; on the back it said "CAUTION: EASILY INFLAMMABLE."

Now we come to the SuperFollower: "We'd like to move this item from here to there."

"That is a great idea," he'll say. "I am really proud of you for coming up with that idea. But you know what? It's not the right time; the people are not ready yet. Let's wait and see. Let us think about it a bit more."

What is the (- - - **I**) waiting for? Consensus. He wants to be sure there is political support for the idea before he acts on it.

What you have to do is say, "We want to move the item from here to there, and we've already talked to everybody in the department and they are all in favor."

"Oh, all right, let's move it then!"

Each of the mismanagers will give you resistance to change. In contrast, if you go to the Deadwood and say, "We would like to move New York to the Sahara," he'll say, "Sure. Great idea. Let's do it." He'll show *no* resistance.

Boren's Laws:
First law: When in charge, ponder.
Second law: When in trouble, delegate.
Third law: When in doubt, mumble.

THOMAS L. MARTIN, JR.

Immediately he'll start preparing a file to document his efforts, and that file will soon be so thick that it would take a battery of lawyers to prove he didn't do the job. A year later, if you ask him how the project to move New York to the Sahara is going, he will tell you, "We hired consultants. We have researched the subject; we have a study. We have a committee working on it."

Everything is being done except one thing: Not a pebble from New York has been moved anywhere. Nevertheless, the Deadwood's survival is totally protected and guaranteed by his labyrinthine documentation. This is why he is so difficult to eradicate. How can you fire someone who does all the right things and always agrees with you?

The irony is, the person I'm describing is every manager's favorite subordinate! You say, "How's it going?" He says, "No problem; everything is fine." You give him an assignment; he says, "Sure." This is the person you always wanted, right? You don't want someone who says, "No, that can't be done," or "I have no time," or "That's the wrong thing to do." You want someone who says, "Fine," no matter what.

But think about it: Where is the quietest place in the city? The cemetery. Nothing is happening there. There are no more complaints.

In fact, one way to identify the Deadwood in your organization is to go and ask, "Any problems?" The one who says, "No problem, everything is fine" – that's the first indication.

Then test him. Give him an assignment that you know *should not* be done and *cannot* be done. And if he says, "Fine," then you've found him.

No. 4: Deadwood's Subordinates

From the Lone Ranger you get gofers; from the Bureaucrat, yes-yes clerks. From Arsonists, claques; from SuperFollowers, informers.

Who works for Deadwood?

Other Deadwood.

Why?

First of all, Deadwood's hiring practices reflect his strategy for survival. He favors not-so-bright subordinates, even to the point of promoting those who produce less than he does.

"First-class managers hire first-class people.
Second-class managers hire third-class people."

Anonymous

Also, any subordinates who wish to grow and develop are completely frustrated by a Deadwood manager. He does not grow, nor does he let anyone under him grow. Either the Deadwood's subordinates get out, or they mentally die in their jobs, becoming Deadwood too. The disease can even spread beyond the subsystem in which it exists, as other people see how the Deadwood survives and think, "Well, I can do the same. I can do nothing and survive or even get promoted." In one organization I worked with, an employee was fired, and a Deadwood employee, bewildered, complained: "I don't know *why* they fired him. He didn't *do* anything!"

Even those who are not quite Deadwood themselves can create full-fledged Deadwood. The gofers who work for the Lone Ranger and the yes-yes clerks who work for the Bureaucrat become Deadwood. The members of the claque who work for the Arsonist eventually learn to suppress their own aspirations. They learn to make lots of noise but do very little: They become Deadwood.

The SuperFollower's subordinates become Deadwood, too. They are never sure what really needs to be done, and they become sick and tired of the politics, so they give up and just follow. Where? Nowhere, since the SuperFollower gives no direction.

Deadwood spreads exactly like a cancer: No complaints, everything is fine for years and years before you finally see the problem. You don't know you have it, it's difficult to eradicate, and in the meantime it's spreading. By the time you catch it, it might be too late. Deadwood is a malignancy in organizations.

The worst disaster is to have Deadwood at the top of an organization. The Deadwood executive is not going to stretch and produce more or different things. He no longer wants to change; he is happy with what was previously accomplished. Although such management sometimes tries to disguise itself as conservative, it is in fact moribund. Having Deadwood at the top is fatal to an organization.

ORIGIN OF THE SPECIES

What causes Deadwood? People give all kinds of answers. Some say it's nepotism: being hired or promoted because of your connections or family, not because of what you know or what you can do. Others say it's management by seniority, a tradition in which the next most senior person will get promoted whether he knows what he's doing or not. Other reasons might be lack of management appraisal or lack of training.

In my opinion, all these explanations are legitimate. But I don't believe they are the main reasons why Deadwood occurs.

What should stand out by now is that all of the previous four types of mismanagement – the (**P** - - -), or Lone Ranger; the (- **A**- -), or Bureaucrat; the (- - **E** -), or Arsonist; and the (- - - **I**), or SuperFollower are *already three-quarters Deadwood* (- - - -)! Their capabilities are neither wide-ranging nor flexible enough to allow them to adapt to new situations. So sooner or later, they're going to burn out.

Let's look at the Lone Ranger, for instance. How does he become Deadwood? The Lone Ranger works very hard: first one in, last one out, *no* time for meetings, no time for training subordinates: there's too much to do right *now*.

Who else does he not train and develop? *Himself.*

An ad for one of my seminars once said, "If you have no time to come to this seminar, that is the best reason why you should come." That ad was directed especially toward the Lone Ranger type, who is always claiming he has no time for training. Thus, 20 years down the road, he's not a person with 20 years of experience. He's a person with one year of experience – repeated 20 times.

He's so busy pushing that rock, so busy (**P**)-ing, that he has no time to look around and see that while he's been moving the rock out of the pathway, the world has changed. There might be a new highway nearby. The rock may not be relevant anymore. When the Lone Ranger sees a task, he puts his head down and starts pushing ahead as hard as he can, with all his energies in one direction. The fact that his head is down and he can't see what's in front of him – that should bother him, but it doesn't. Technology passes him by, and eventually he becomes technically incompetent and unable to produce the same results as in the past. He keeps pushing and pushing, but as time passes he might easily be pushing the wrong thing.

What happens to a (**P - - -**) who has never bothered to learn new ways of doing things, who keeps doing the wrong things, the old things? The Lone Ranger of today is the Deadwood of tomorrow.

Ironically, this new Deadwood was once your best (**P**)roducer – the person you were most confident of and pleased with! And because you remember that he was your best (**P**)roducer, you are reluctant to fire him. You, as his manager, might even feel guilty and responsible for his failures.

There is an especially tragic quality to the fate of the Lone Ranger who becomes Deadwood. The Lone Ranger starts out being a very hard-working individual. He dedicates his life to the company and usually neglects his family. But his short-term orientation keeps him so frenetically busy that he has no time to keep up with innovations in his field, to develop himself.

Years later, he is still working hard, but the results are not what they used to be. He has become obsolete. When the time comes to fire the non-performers, the Lone Ranger may be the first to go. And he is devastated. He worked so hard! He dedicated his life to the company. He hardly knows his own children. He has had few experiences beyond his work. And what is the reward for such loyalty and dedication? He is out on the street in his old age, looking for a job.

But who would want him? His skills are antiquated; his capacity to learn new techniques has atrophied. He's useless!

In Arthur Miller's play *Death of a Salesman*, Willy Loman is the salesman who has become obsolete, whose increasingly futile efforts bring fewer and fewer results. Willy reacts by drifting in and out of the past, reliving his best moments and ignoring reality. In the end, inevitably, he is fired, and he cannot understand why. In the opinion of his company, he has become Deadwood.[2]

How does a Bureaucrat (**- A - -**) become Deadwood? He loses his ability to (**A**).

The Bureaucrat has always been too focused on establishing controls. He, too, easily loses sight of the big picture. His rigidity almost guarantees that a systemic upheaval will crack him. Any major unexpected shift in the internal or external business environment will reduce him to Deadwood.

For example, the Bureaucrat manages by the book. If you want to destroy him professionally, you merely have to change the book.

An easy way to do that is to bring in new technology: New computers and systems, new manuals, new methods and procedures. The Bureaucrat, who is inflexible and lacks the style needed to adapt, will quickly surrender, throwing up his hands as if to say, "The world has passed me by; I don't understand what's going on anymore. Do whatever you want. I can't follow anymore; I can't catch up." He simply gives up, telling himself that "old dogs can't learn new tricks." (And please note: you don't have to be 60 or 70 or 80 to be too old. Some people become too old at the age of 25.)

When he is overwhelmed by too much change and can no longer successfully organize, delegate, or coordinate, the Bureaucrat becomes Deadwood. He has lost the capacity to learn and grow in his job; he only knows how to go through the same old paces he's already familiar with.

When an (- **A** - -) burns out, the consequences are usually more widespread than when a (**P** - - -) burns out. The (- **A** - -)'s department suffers a seizure, much the way a poorly timed engine might freeze up. Why? Because now there are at least two systems at work: the new one, and the old one that the Bureaucrat will not let go of. Efficiency goes to hell, and when, inevitably, the chaos becomes too obvious to sweep under the rug, he will yield in order to avoid being fired. He'll let whatever happens happen. He becomes Deadwood.

Now, how does the Arsonist burn out? He starts one fire too many and is finally spread too thin. Like the straw that broke the camel's back, that last fire can destroy the entire organization, spewing ash and destruction everywhere as it burns out of control. Meanwhile, the Arsonist watches helplessly, too overwhelmed to know how or where to reestablish control. Very often, the Arsonist never really comprehends how or why the company got into trouble.

I've talked to some (**E**)ntrepreneurs who have created multimillion-dollar companies and then gone bankrupt, climbed back up and gone bankrupt, two or three times in a row. I've asked them, "What was the common denominator each time?" And they say, "I didn't listen to anyone. I was feeling too good about my achievement. I started believing my own press releases. We were growing, I was at the top of the mountain, and I felt so confident in my abilities that I would start another fire, develop *another* business and *another* deal and *another* agreement. I felt *invincible*.

"There was so much excitement. And people won't dare to tell you 'no,' because they know you already think they're idiots, and if they say 'no' it will just *confirm* that they're idiots. So they're forced to say, 'Sure.' They cannot deny your success; so they cross their fingers and hope that if you could do it once, maybe you can do it a hundred times."

They do worry, of course. In the corridor, they are whispering to each other, "My God, what should we do? How do we stop this unguided missile?" The smart ones resign ahead of the fiasco they know is coming. Those who don't have the option or the courage to resign become Deadwood: they clap and call "Bravo!" while whispering to each other, "We are in *deep* doodoo."

But believing himself to be invincible, the (- - **E** -) behaves according to what he *wants* the reality to be or what he thinks it *should* be, rather than what it really *is*. He overreacts promiscuously to opportunities. Every change, every opportunity is an opportunity, until one more opportunity becomes a threat.

Arsonists, like adolescents, are always trying to test their limits. They know where the limits are only after they have crossed them. They actually like to court disaster, almost asking for it, just to see where the limits are. But sometimes they cross a boundary that is critical and disastrous – and irreparable. Then they are doomed. They go bankrupt. They lose everything they have built, and they never saw it coming.

When that happens, the Arsonist often loses his *chutzpah*, his nerve. He loses his gift for creative, proactive decision-making. He no longer leads the organization; he no longer takes risks. From then on, he just says, "Uh huh, uh huh," to everything: "Maybe it's right, maybe it's wrong; I don't know anymore."

Sometimes he's bought out by a big, cash-heavy company because he's run out of money after starting too many projects too fast. The new owners give him some kind of big long title, like "Senior VP for long-range planning," which basically means "Sit down and shut up and let us clean up the mess you have created." He's still got a lot of ideas and a fire in his belly, but he's lost confidence and has no credibility: nobody's listening anymore. The owners appoint a big (**A**) to control the organization, and the Arsonist becomes de facto Deadwood.

There is another possible outcome: If the Arsonist, the organization's "big wheel," keeps continually, incessantly, and unpredictably changing direction, without waiting for the smaller wheels to catch up, eventually the axle breaks down and nothing moves. The Arsonist, oblivious, keeps moving and turning on his own, but the others do not follow. Although he still has ideas, he's lost the confidence of subordinates, bankers, suppliers, investors – even his own spouse doesn't trust him anymore. He is marching forward but alone.

Soon, understandably, the Arsonist becomes paranoid. On the one hand, his subordinates complain about how hard they work, and they *do* seem to be working hard. (They *have* to look like they are working hard; if they don't, he will create new crises for them to deal with.)

On the other hand, nothing gets accomplished: The Arsonist's projects and instructions never reach fruition. Because the (- - **E** -)'s subordinates expect him to change directions anyway, they are reluctant to commit themselves to any specific project.

Trying to resolve this contradiction, the Arsonist begins to believe that there are two realities – the one he observes and another whose existence he suspects. He starts looking for a scapegoat. His confidence disappears, he loses his nerve, and in extreme cases he becomes paralyzed and unable to act: He becomes Deadwood.

How does a SuperFollower (- - - I) become Deadwood? He becomes Deadwood when there is a problem that must be solved *now*. There is pressure and crisis, and he no longer has time to maneuver by saying, "Well, you didn't understand what I wanted to say," or, "I really meant to say ...," or, "Let's wait for the next committee to decide," or, "Let's postpone. ..." The problem is: There is no more time! A decision must be made NOW! There is a problem NOW! Suddenly the (- - - I)'s customary political strategies are insufficient.

Whatever social sensitivity and communication skills he once had have dissipated, and the conflicts have become so overwhelming that they exceed his ability to (I)ntegrate them. Having lost his ability to perform the only role he excelled at, the SuperFollower cannot provide what is needed. People stop listening to the SuperFollower and no longer follow him, and he becomes a plain follower. Over time, his importance in the organization diminishes, and he is pushed aside and ignored. What emerges then is a new clique, young Turks who are prepared to overthrow the current management, make decisions, and fulfill the organization's needs.

THE COMMON DENOMINATOR

What is the common denominator in all four cases?

CHANGE!!!!!

The Lone Ranger and the Bureaucrat cannot adapt to new ways of doing new things. The Arsonist reacts promiscuously to change, shooting at every target until he's used up all the ammunition. The SuperFollower loses his ability to (I)ntegrate because he cannot manipulate under time pressure in the internal political climate.

Deadwood is caused by inflexible styles when subjected to accelerated change.

How the Classic Business Model Produces Deadwood

The day I got my Ph.D. in management at Columbia University, I was walking down the corridor of the school when a crowd of students emerged from one of the classrooms. They'd just finished taking their qualifying exam to become Ph.D. candidates, which means they were approximately one or two years behind me.

"Show me the exam," I said, in my pride and arrogance as a newly minted doctor of philosophy. But when I looked at it I discovered, to my shock, that I couldn't have passed the exam! The day I got my Ph.D., I was already obsolete. Change – in practices, in technology, in theories – had made my nearly brand-new knowledge outdated. It scared the hell out of me. I realized then that it no longer takes 20 years to become obsolete. It may not even take five.

Did you know that 85 percent of all scientists who have ever lived are alive today? We are experiencing the highest rate of change that mankind has ever known. And what are the repercussions of this accelerated change?

Let me make an analogy to the body. Our bodies developed over billions of years into what they are today, by adapting slowly to change. The dinosaurs, which could not adapt to sudden change, perished.

But in the last hundred years, human beings have had to adapt to a much more rapid rate of change – in what we eat, what we breathe, what we do, and how we do it. In some cases, the speed and breadth of these changes have simply overwhelmed the body's capacity to adapt, and it begins to malfunction. It is as if one or another part of the body is saying, "Sorry, I can't change anymore, I can't adapt." Cells begin to mutate or to replicate themselves endlessly, depleting the energy that is necessary to maintain healthy cells. In medicine, that is called cancer. If not stopped, it will metastasize, spreading itself throughout the host, basically devouring the body from the inside out.

Peter's Pretty Pass

"In an occupational hierarchy, neither your own efforts
nor the pull of your patron can help you if the next step
above you is blocked by someone at his level of incompetence."

LAURENCE J. PETER AND RAYMOND HULL,
THE PETER PRINCIPLE

In organizations, the cancer is called Deadwood. Our so-called "modern" organizations are based on a bureaucratic, military model that is structured for adaptation to change over many years. We aren't structured for rapid change, we aren't trained for rapid change, we don't have processes for dealing with rapid change. Thus, we are vulnerable to developing corporate cancer – Deadwood – which reduces our productivity and profitability.

LOSING THE ROCK

How does the structure of a so-called "modern" organization exacerbate this problem? Corporate structure is traditionally a pyramid, a hierarchy: Somebody is at the top and supervisors are in the middle, with an acceptable span of control.

The irony is that it's not modern at all: The Pharaohs in ancient Egypt probably had their armies organized that way. Even our earliest ancestors, the monkeys, form cultures that are structured hierarchically – top monkeys and lower-level monkeys.

This pyramid structure builds layers that actually prevent and inhibit change. That's because it was never designed to facilitate change. Historically, the purpose and function of a pyramid structure has been to foster the efficient implementation of orders.

What layers am I talking about? Let's look at the pyramid. We know that the four roles of management are (**PAEI**). Now, which of the four roles is performed almost exclusively at the bottom of the hierarchy? That would be (**P**): (**P**)roduction managers are expected to come in early, leave late, and work like hell. Nobody wants their ideas, nobody wants their creativity or their (**I**)ntegration. Don't try to unionize here; just work like hell, (**P**) all day long! In a word, they are (**P**)eons.

What do we have in the middle? Layers and layers of (**A**). And as organizations grow, they keep adding more (**A**).

Classical management theory worries about how many workers a manager can manage – the so-called span of control. I, on the contrary, worry about how many managers one worker can carry.

You remember the "rock," in my analogy of the five friends, that created the need for management? Now, by adding layers of (**A**), we're adding people whose task is to communicate to the people who are pushing the rock. We're also adding people who are going to plan how they're going to communicate to those who are pushing the rock; and we're adding people who are going to lead those who are planning what is being communicated, and others who are going to control those who are leading those who are communicating to those who are planning....

Do you see what's happening? There are so many people managing the guy who's pushing that rock that nobody sees the rock anymore. And the danger is that these new layers of people – the coordinators, supervisors, organizers, and leaders – will start to believe that what *they* are doing is the rock. They forget the *real* rock: Satisfying the client's needs.

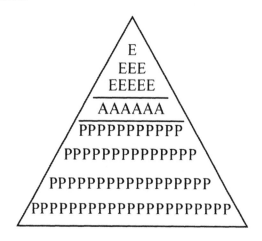

What is the desired role at the top of the pyramid? This is strategic planning, vision – the (**E**) role.

So you have (**P**), you have (**A**), you have (**E**). Where is the (**I**)? Usually (**I**) is positioned somewhere in the middle, in a department called Human Resources Development or something similar. When there's a problem, they're the ones who put together a touchy-feely meeting. But they're not on the Executive Committee. The company makes concessions to (**I**) maybe two times a year: The first one is called the Christmas party and the other the company picnic. Done. That's (**I**).

The pyramid is very neat, isn't it? On top is (**E**), who makes the decisions and points out the direction; below are those who enforce the decisions, and at the bottom, way down there, are the performers. So where's the problem?

In order to answer that question, it's important to distinguish between two types of decision-making: Programmed and non-programmed.

Programmed decisions are decisions that were already taken, decided. For a predetermined stimulus, there is a predetermined response.

An example of that would be driving home. How many times have you had the experience after work where you get into your car, turn the engine on, and the next thing you know you're in front of your garage? How did you drive there? You don't remember.

What happened is that your brain is very efficient; when it picks up certain repetitive patterns it programs the correct response, and then you don't have to think about it anymore. It's called habit.

When you learned how to drive, you got programmed: Red light stop, green light go. Do this, do that. In time you began to respond automatically even to certain sounds: If you were driving a stick shift, when the noise became more grinding, you shifted gears.

Your brain is like a computer: For a predetermined stimulus, it offers a predetermined response. Your eyes are the sensing mechanism, your hands and your feet are the responding mechanism, there is a little memory bank with a program called "Drive Home from Office," and when the eyes or ears see or hear something for which a response has been programmed, you automatically make a change.

And what are *you* doing while the brain is making its programmed way home? You are thinking about non-programmed things. What are non-programmed things? The decisions you haven't made yet.

Now let us assume your wife tells you to buy some milk on the way home. When you get home you get hell. Why? You forgot to buy the milk. What happened? You drove home in a programmed way, which allowed you to do some other non-programmed thinking at the same time – but the program had no "Get milk" programmed into it. So you "forgot."

In a well-managed company, a typical programmed decision would be inventory control. You have previously decided how much inventory you need to have in the warehouse, so when you hit a certain minimum of inventory, it's time to order again.

Your business manual is also all programs: How to produce, how to sell, how to prepare a budget.

A non-programmed decision is, for instance, "How do we penetrate a new market?" Of course, if we are in the consulting business of penetrating new markets, then that becomes part of the programming. But if it's the first time you're doing it, it's non-routine, it's non-repetitive, thus it's non-programmed.

The four management roles can be classified in terms of the type of decision-making they require. (**A**), for example, is associated almost exclusively with programmed decision-making: Here's what you do; here's how you do it. By the book, deliberately programmed, because you want to repeat success by routinization.

What else is programmed? (**P**)! Have you ever stopped a telemarketing salesman in the midst of making his pitch? Some poor guys have to start all over again from the beginning! Why? Because what do we do when we train salesmen? We program them.

We spend millions if not billions of dollars to program people, with training and seminars, so that all people will do the same things exactly the same way.

Now, when a new manager comes in and wants to make changes, he finds resistance. But who do you think created this resistance to change? The company itself did! The company spent millions of dollars to train people to be so programmed that they cannot change easily.

I once saw a book on the subject of change that had the following artwork on its cover:

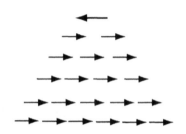

Next point.

If somebody has a beautiful idea or a problem down there at the bottom, can they solve it down there? No. It has to go up to the top for approval. And how easy is it to get through to the top – even if there are suggestion boxes and an open-door policy and management by walking around? Those factors might make a difference, but not a big one. That's why the people down there say, "Forget it. If I have a good idea I'll make it work outside. I will moonlight. I'll start a business in my garage after working hours, or I'll resign as soon as I can and go somewhere else. In the meantime I'll just do whatever they tell me to do, the minimum I can get away with, and get my salary and that's it."

How about if the change is initiated at the top? After all, the job of top management is to visualize the future and lead the change. But what is the chance that (**E**) will cross barriers and barriers and barriers of (**A**) to make that change happen? It is going to be very difficult, like trying to conceive while using multiple condoms.

The (**P**) isn't expected to do (**E**); the (**A**) isn't expected to do (**E**). We have deliberately created organizations that support a specialization in roles and a hierarchy of roles, and that makes us inflexible.

Some organizations are actually born inflexible–they're called government agencies and they are *born* without a head. The organization is all (**A**) and (**P**). You know where the (**E**) is? It is with the politicians. Government agencies have no discretionary power. The politicians have all the authority to decide on change. As a matter of fact, those who work for the government are called public servants, or public (**A**)dministrators. The infinitive "to (**A**)dminister" derives from the word "to serve."

Those who (**A**)dminister do not decide. Instead, they serve whatever was decided. That's fine, but the result is a bureaucracy; what do you expect?

What do politicians do when there is a need for change? They make what is called political appointments. These are positions in the hierarchy directly under and report to the head of the department.

What does that look like?

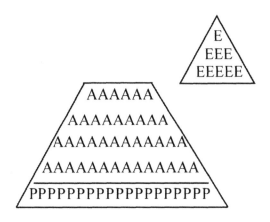

I have concluded that the organizational structure, the hierarchy, or so-called pyramid, as it has been developed and practiced for hundreds, if not thousands, of years, is simply not structured for rapid change. It is structured for the implementation of routine decisions; for efficiency and short-term effectiveness – *not* for long-term effectiveness or long-term efficiency.

It is linear. It assumes that the world is flat. Energy flows only one way – from the top down. Open doors, walking around, and president's workouts are all merely bypasses to arteries that have been clogged by design. And in this clogged structure, Deadwood flourishes.

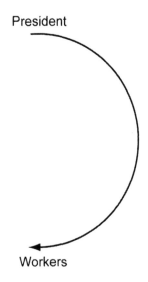

Energy cannot flow top down and bottom up in the same channels. Thus, organizations must have parallel structures.

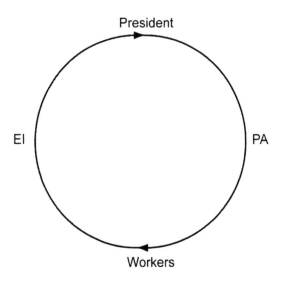

How to do this is a subject for another book. At the Adizes Institute we have formulated and installed such structures in hundreds of companies. Those companies have been able to achieve sustainable accelerated, change without the side effects of Deadwood.

WHY (A)S PROLIFERATE IN ORGANIZATIONS

When your company was young, you had a lot of (**P**)'s. Everybody was out (**P**)-ing like crazy, because the only way to survive was by pushing that rock to satisfy the clients for whom you started the company in the first place. In a young company, there is usually very little (**A**): one secretary, a bookkeeper, and maybe one supervisor; that's all the (**A**) you get. That's why young companies are relatively disorganized. Very little (**A**) and a lot of (**E**): Constantly changing, adapting, moving.

What happens over time is very interesting. The (**A**) grows. The company adds another supervisor, another coordinator. The organization grows according to Parkinson's Law: The job has not changed, but the number of people who need to control and monitor the process is constantly growing. And what is the first thing they do? They push the (**E**) out, and then they push the (**P**) out. Eventually, what you have is an organization with so much (**A**) that it becomes moribund.

(E)s Come and Go; (A)s Accumulate

There is an Israeli expression: "Friends go and come; enemies accumulate." If we rephrase it slightly, we can see another way that companies lose their (**E**). When your organization is small, usually you have a lot of (**P**), as well as some (**A**) and (**E**). But as the company grows, look what happens: The ratio between (**E**) and (**A**) starts to decline, until eventually it reaches a point where the (**E**) is lonely at the top of the hierarchy and isn't even taken seriously anymore; he's treated like an Arsonist.

I've talked to many founders of companies who wistfully remember the days when over breakfast they could make a decision—and get it implemented. But now the same decision—even when you have the same hundred-percent ownership—takes three months to get approved. What happened? (**A**)*!!!!!* Unless it is monitored and controlled, (**A**) squeezes out (**E**) and eventually (**P**).

The organization now consists of people who have forgotten what the rock is, who believe the rock is to (**A**). But (**A**) is actually management of the people pushing the rock, which means (**A**) is *not* the rock. (**A**)dministration is there to serve its clients, not itself.

When (**E**) has become localized in a very limited space and is monopolized there, (**E**) becomes an endangered species. In fact, there are some languages in which the word "Entrepreneur" doesn't exist anymore. I know this because one of my books, *How to Solve the Mismanagement Crisis*,[3] has been translated into 22 languages, and in some of those languages the translators have told me, "We cannot translate some of your words."

I say, "Which words, for instance?"

They say, "The word 'Entrepreneur.'"

"Entrepreneur!" I scream. "How can that be?"

But it is true. In Swedish, for example, according to the translator, the word "Entrepreneur" existed hundreds of years ago, in old Swedish, but there is no such word in modern Swedish. "Then use the *old* word!" I insisted. "Let us rejuvenate it. Maybe by rejuvenating the word we will start rejuvenating the phenomenon."

"Entrepreneur" is a French word, but oddly enough, in France today it is used to describe someone who is a real estate developer – as if the phenomenon exists only in the real estate arena.

In Russia during the Communist era, the word "Entrepreneur" was used to describe someone on his way to jail. It was a synonym for the German word *spekulant*, which means someone who benefits from speculation and thus exploitation–someone who does not add value; who is, in fact, a menace to society.

If the word is disappearing, then the phenomenon must also be disappearing. (**E**)ntrepreneurs are the endangered species of the industrial, (**A**)-oriented society. Now you have to pay millions of dollars in salary and stock options for an (**E**) top executive! Why? The price is going up because the quantity is becoming scarce. The more we become over-trained, over-educated, over-programmed and thus over-bureaucratized, the fewer (**E**) types we are able to find, support, and nourish.

Because the structurer of a typical organization stresses specialization of roles, we have little opportunity to develop well-rounded skills or to develop in areas in which we are weak. Consequently, we are losing our ability to handle change easily and promptly. For example, if a (**P**) wants to advance, he has to learn (**A**) skills–from scratch! If he cannot learn to perform the (**A**) role quickly enough, he becomes Deadwood. I knew a famous surgeon who became the managing director of a large hospital. Because he was incapable of (**A**)dministering it, he became a Deadwood (**A**)dministrator – and the hospital lost a top surgeon.

This happens frequently in high-tech companies. When the company starts to grow, the inventor/founder needs to learn to (**A**)dminister: He needs to see to it that the company hires the right people of the appropriate diversity, has salary (**A**)dministration as needed, puts safety policies into effect, monitors the accounting, etc. – all tasks that he not only hates but is incapable of doing. And what happens? We lose a top-notch technologist and gain a Deadwood (**A**)dministrator.

What about an (**A**) who is promoted further up the ladder? He immediately needs to perform the (**E**) role. For 35 years he's been an (**A**); how can he be expected to become an (**E**) overnight? He can't. People usually repeat the behavior for which they've been rewarded. Being an (**A**) worked for him – so why change? He will repeat what he knows and what worked for him, until he becomes Deadwood. He is (A)-ing in a job that calls for (**E**). He is dysfunctional. He is not performing. He is blocking rather than leading change. Laurence J. Peter and Raymond Hull called this phenomenon "the Peter Principle": "In a hierarchically structured administration, people tend to be promoted up to their "level of incompetence."[4]

The Peter Principle

"In a hierarchy, every employee tends to rise
to his maximum level of incompetence.
"Corollary 1: Given enough time, and assuming
the existence of enough ranks, each employee rises
to and remains at his level of incompetence.
"Corollary 2: In time, every post tends to be
occupied by an employee who is incompetent to
carry out its duties."

LAURENCE J. PETER AND RAYMOND HULL,
THE PETER PRINCIPLE

Deadwood almost never leave an organization on their own; either they die on the job, or they retire or are fired. They aren't missed, but by the time they go the organization is usually dead as well. No purposeful activity, no creativity, no (**I**)ntegration of people is evident.

The causes of Deadwood are woven tightly into the structure of the organization. The danger is inherent. If organizations do not restructure themselves to remove dashes in their managers' (**PAEI**) codes and encourage flexibility, they can easily develop Deadwood, the cancer that will eventually bring their demise.

NOTES

1. Bell, Gerald: *The Achievers* (Chapel Hill, N.C.: Preston Hill, 1973), Chapter 7.

2. Miller, Arthur: *Death of a Salesman: Certain Private Conversations in Two Acts and a Requiem* (New York: Viking, 1949).

3. Adizes, Ichak: *How to Solve the Mismanagement Crisis* (Santa Monica, Calif.: Adizes Institute, 1985).

4. Peter, Laurence J.; and Raymond Hull: *The Peter Principle: Why Things Always Go Wrong* (New York: William Morrow & Co., 1969).

Performing Several Roles, But Not All of Them

We have seen what happens when one managerial role is performed exclusively. When (**E**) is the only role performed, for example, you have an Arsonist, a person who is solely interested in creating new plans and new projects.

However, when the (**E**) role is coupled with some other managerial role, you will have a creative manager whose creativity is focused on his second sphere of excellence. For example, if the person is a (**P - E -**), he may be an inventor who is always working to improve his innovations.

When a manager's (**E**) is coupled with (**A**), his creativity is oriented toward (**A**)dministrative systems. A (**pAEI**) would give us a leader and possibly a good consultant or systems analyst, someone who uses his creativity to improve the control systems of an organization. But if he is an (**- AE -**), he will just be a Pain in the Neck. Because of the blanks in his managerial code, an (**- AE -**) can only be a mismanager. In contrast, a (**pAEi**) is a typical manager who has strengths (**AE**) and weaknesses (**pi**).

When (**E**) and (**I**) are coupled, the SuperFollower disappears. This manager's (**E**) is oriented toward the (I)ntegration of ideas. However, if he performs only these two roles exclusively – (**EI**) – then he will be a Demagogue. If, on the other hand, his (P) is also strong – (**PaEI**)–he could be a successful statesman, while a (**paEI**) will end up not in history books but in academia, teaching or writing analyses of what the (**PaEI**) statesman did or should have done.

There are ten combinations of roles that appear frequently, creating ten styles of mismanagement. These styles are the subject of this chapter.

Although in the following archetypes I will describe only mismanagement styles, it should be easy for you to envision the corresponding management style for each: just remove the negatives. To further imagine this type of mismanager as a leader, add excellence in (I)ntegration to his code and try to visualize him as (I)ntegrating specifically for the other role in which he excels. For instance, a (**paEI**) will integrate with a vision, while a (**PaeI**) will integrate for some immediate task that needs to be done.

THE SLAVE DRIVER, (PA - -)

The Slave Driver is oriented toward achievement, results, and control. He is interested in efficiency and effectiveness, in *what* people do and in *how* they do it. If he were at least minimally competent at the (**E**) and (**I**) roles, he would fit the profile of a managerial type that I call the Taskmaster. However, because he lacks (**E**) and (**I**), he is neither creative nor people oriented.

This autocratic manager has a very mechanistic view of the organization. His plans and work are highly organized and systematized. He relies heavily upon precedents and past experiences. His strong (**P**) orientation means he focuses intensely on whatever task he happens to be working on; he also makes everyone else work hard. His strong (**A**) makes him efficiency oriented and concerned with control over processes. He prefers top down communication. The Slave Driver is frequently found in the military. A company with too many managers of this type is in danger of stagnating.

How does the Slave Driver differ from the Lone Ranger? Unlike the (**P - - -**), he excels and delights in putting things in order, and he also demands regular staff meetings. Unlike the Bureaucrat (**- A - -**), who cares little about results as long as the process is implemented correctly, the Slave Driver values the ends as well as the means. In his book *Breach of Faith*,[1] Theodore H. White quoted this statement by White House chief of staff for President Nixon, H.R. Haldeman, which exemplifies the Slave Driver's attitude or may be he was a Taskmaster (**PAei**), the difference is only one of degree: "I've never concerned myself with the issues; I'm a political mechanic. I work programs, not issues, not speeches, not phrases.... I'm simply putting it all together." Bob was an Associate of the Adizes Institute, as well as a personal friend, in the last days of his life, and he is greatly missed. I once asked him: "Bob, how did you manage the White House staff?" His response was typical for a Slave Driver or Taskmaster: "By fear!!!"

The Slave Driver is inflexible and opinionated. Getting the job done right, *his* way, is all-important. He pays careful attention to details, deadlines, and procedures, and little attention to people. He has no sympathy, and he accepts no excuses. His impersonal, businesslike approach makes him appear distant and inhuman, like a machine; he is not the person to ask favors of.

On the other hand, his behavior is highly predictable, which makes him easy to cope with as long as one is willing to be enslaved. His subordinates always know exactly where they stand with him. They fear him, but they can learn to live with him once they understand that to the Slave Driver, other people are simply tools for getting the job done. Subordinates who hate uncertainty admire him and see him as a true leader.

Ironically, however, the Slave Driver is himself a tool in the hands of others. He drives his slaves in the service of other people's goals; he has no agenda of his own. He is basically a loyal, dedicated, and hardworking servant who carries out his orders efficiently. In order to please his bosses, he accepts tasks blindly and carries them out blindly.

The Slave Driver is despised by those who possess any spark of independence and self respect. The stifling, inhumane, "work only" atmosphere he creates is intolerable to some, and they eventually quit. But others find the security and certainty he offers to be an acceptable trade-off for their enslavement. After some time, they even resist being freed, because this would introduce uncertainty into their lives.

How does a manager become a (**PA- -**)? Usually by being promoted, for such a person probably starts out as a strong achiever with a latent need for power. He works hard and achieves results, and his success as a (**P**) leads naturally to a managerial position. As a manager, however, he is still dominated by his results orientation, except that now he adds to it the role of (**A**)dministrating, or controlling, so that his subordinates will achieve results as well. Given this opportunity to manage others, his need to exercise power comes into full bloom.

Without the promotion, he would have remained a pure (**P**). However, the (**A**), (**E**), and (**I**) deficiencies that were latent and benign when the Slave Driver was an employee, or "slave," become dysfunctional and malignant once he is promoted to a managerial position. The result? A Slave Driver.

The Slave Driver is impatient with himself and others. "Keep moving" is the feeling he imparts to those around him. His speech is terse, his penetrating eyes are ice-cold, his movements are abrupt. He often cuts people off in the middle of their sentences and finishes the sentence himself. If he is somehow prevented from interrupting, he gets angry (not only at the person who's speaking but also at himself for losing control of the conversation), and will act out his impatience and displeasure by "freezing out" the speaker: He fixes his eyes on the person who is talking, locks his jaws tightly, and remains utterly motionless until the other person gets the message and shuts up.

If the speaker happens to be someone who is higher up on the corporate ladder and cannot be frozen out, the Slave Driver will use body language to disrupt the conversation – for example, rocking his whole body in an up and down motion: First up on his toes, then down on his heels. When he is up on his toes, he looks dangerously off balance, as if he might jump or fall forward. When he lands on his heels he clicks them together, sometimes also smacking his lips or clicking his tongue for emphasis.

In managerial literature, the Slave Driver is analogous to the "Commander" style described by Gerald Bell.[2] The Commander is determined to regulate *all* of the events that occur within his realm. He blames mistakes on subordinates. He dislikes ambiguity and uncertainty, and comforts himself by dividing everything and everyone into categories. (It has been said, jokingly, that there are "two types of people in the world: The type who dichotomize everything, and the others.")

Commanders tend to stress short-term goals almost as much as ultimate objectives. They communicate one way: Down! They will tell you what to do and talk about how to get the job done, but that is all.

Bell claims that Commanders perform best in a relatively stable environment. Given clear cut tasks that can be accomplished in an orderly, precise manner, a Commander will assert his control, dominate the routines, dominate the subordinates, and concentrate on the means to the end.

An organization run by a Slave Driver lacks creativity and is unable to readily adapt to changes in the environment. Although short-run efficiency is good, morale is low and turnover is high. Promotions are won by those who don't cause problems; thus creativity – which tends to promote change – is hampered.

When the (**PA - -**) leaves an organization, there is a noticeable decline in (P)roductivity. People are apt to strike, slack off, and show similar manifestations of rebellion and relief.

What happens if the Slave Driver is also capable of (**I**)ntegrating ideas and people? We would then have our next combined style of mismanagement, (**PA-I**), the Benevolent Prince.

THE BENEVOLENT PRINCE, (PA-I)

The Benevolent Prince combines three managerial roles: (P)roducing, (**A**)dministrating, and (**I**)ntegrating. He is interested in short-term results, (**P**), and efficient systems of control, (**A**), and he is also capable of uniting people to implement the decisions and the systems, (**I**).

Whereas the Slave Driver (**PA- -**) simply gets people working, the Benevolent Prince allows others to present and discuss ideas, although he makes the final decision himself. In one organization, the (**PA-I**) would listen to ideas, decide what was desirable, obtain agreement, then proceed as a Slave Driver toward the goals. Since the ideas were acceptable to the people in the organization, this Benevolent Prince was powerful and effective.

The Benevolent Prince is distant and impersonal. His subordinates worship him and work hard to get the job done the way he wants it done. The subordinates have no ideas of their own, but neither does he. He is not a king. If the Benevolent Prince were even minimally competent in the (**E**) role, he could be a Tactical Leader (**PaeI**). But, lacking (**E**), he is just a prince who is able to get people to do the job amicably.

The box in front of the Slave Driver that is drumming says:
"Suggestion Box"
Drawing by Chas. Adams: 1976 The New Yorker Magazine, Inc.

Lacking (**E**), the Benevolent Prince also lacks charisma: thus he is not really capable of uniting people around his vision for any length of time. As a small time implementation (**I**)ntegrator, the Benevolent

Prince exerts a positive impact in the short run. But after he leaves the organization, his followers will disintegrate as a group over time, because they have no ideas, (**E**), to (**I**)ntegrate them, only an implementation system that slowly becomes obsolete.

Without ideas of his own, the Benevolent Prince functions as a team member (**AI**) who brings the ideas of others to fruition (**P**). This description of Cyrus Vance, from a *New York Times* article, is characteristic of a Benevolent Prince. I have noted the roles where they appear in this description:

"In the Pentagon he developed a reputation as a good manager, an implementer of policy [**A**], and a man able to get along with the military [**I**] even when Defense Secretary McNamara's relations with the military began to sour. ... Some of those who worked with him in the past consider him to be too much of a consensus man, waiting for positions and pressures to develop before taking a stand [**I**]. He does not jump in right away, but comes in before the outcome is clear, particularly on an issue with moral aspects [**I**]. ... Some maintained that Mr. Vance is not imaginative [no **E**].... He is described as a good technician [**P**], a loyal team player [**I**].... His style in the past has been to let the White House take the lead [no **E**] ... the professional diplomats who know Mr. Vance expect him to run a well organized department [**A**], but to maintain a low profile [no **E**]. ... Mr. Carter stressed [Vance's] competence rather than his conceptual brilliance or policy innovation [no **E**]. ... Vance is a superb technocrat [**P**] with an incisive executive mind who executed presidential policy [**A**]...." [3]

The role mentioned most frequently (four times) is (**I**). (**A**) is mentioned three times, (**P**) is mentioned two times, and the fact that Vance has no (**E**) is noted four times. Vance's code, then, appears to be either that of a (**PA-I**) – a Benevolent Prince–or a (**PaeI**) – a Shepherd.

What happens if a Benevolent Prince is not oriented or inclined to (**P**)roduce? In that case, we get the Paternalistic Bureaucrat, the next combined style of mismanager.

THE PATERNALISTIC BUREAUCRAT, (- A - I)

This is a nondirective manager, concerned with form and with people – (A) and (I) – but not with ideas and results – (E) and (P). The Paternalistic Bureaucrat might also be called an Open Door Manager. Whatever function he manages, he will work in a more participatory style than most managers. The Paternalistic Bureaucrat seeks to establish controls, but wishes those controls to be agreeable to his people. His concern is with implementing an established system and following established procedures. His (I) enables others to work under him more easily than they would under the Bureaucrat.

The Paternalistic Bureaucrat listens, agrees, and accepts, but only as long as you do not violate any rules! His door is always open, but like the SuperFollower, his apparent willingness to accept the ideas that come through that door is not really sincere. In reality, he has no orientation toward results, no inclination to change anything, and will not tolerate conflict.

The Paternalistic Bureaucrat has regular meetings and lets people talk; he shows concern and interest; he encourages and motivates. Yet his dominant message is always, "We must make the system work the way it's designed to work." Subordinates must get to work on time and must get along with everyone – including, of course, himself.

Training, explanation, and help are more available under the Paternalistic Bureaucrat than under the Bureaucrat, but under both the orientation to (P)roduce is missing. Initially, subordinates like the easygoing atmosphere in an organization headed by a Paternalistic Bureaucrat. The organization seems to run efficiently, and people are very friendly to each other. It is a kind of mutual admiration society. But eventually they realize that their boss's (- A - I) style is creating a stale organization. There is no excitement, no goal orientation, no challenging ideas, no pending changes. Deep disagreements are submerged and never dealt with publicly. The organization has the atmosphere of a resort town for retired people.

The Paternalistic Bureaucrat can only survive in a noncompetitive, unchanging environment. He thrives in government bureaucracies, for example, because he does his job without rocking the boat, thereby minimizing friction. He is basically a friendly Bureaucrat.

But let's change the role combinations around again. When a manager (**P**)roduces results and gets along with people, but lacks vision or a system, we get our next combined mismanagement style, the Little League Coach (**P- - I**).

THE LITTLE LEAGUE COACH, (P - - I)

The Little League Coach excels both at (P)roducing results and at (**I**)ntegrating his subordinates. He is a wonderful facilitator, expert at using compromise to (**P**)roduce short-term results. Although he may be somewhat idealistic and critical, he is a good developer of teams. If he were minimally competent in the (**A**) and (**E**) roles, this manager would be a Shepherd, (**PaeI**), and would probably function well as a people oriented, first line supervisor. He does not concern himself with the external environment to the company – its market, its suppliers, its bankers, its community – and he does not stand on formality. He encourages and supports the people who do the job.

Unlike the Lone Ranger (**P - - -**), the Little League Coach seeks agreement and is people oriented. He rarely establishes a top down command, as the Lone Ranger does. Unlike the SuperFollower, he does (**P**)roduce results. The Little League Coach resembles a youth leader or small town politician. He seeks to generate excitement and then channel that energy into (**P**)roducing results. But this style is successful only in the short-term, because the Little League Coach does not develop a system for follow-through and he has no strategies or large ideas, only short-term tactical goals. Thus, he could never excel as a major-league coach.

If we take away the Little League Coach's orientation toward (**I**)ntegration and make him an (**E**)ntrepreneur instead, what style will we observe?

The Sprouting Founder, (P - E -)

This type of mismanager, who performs only the (P)roducer and (E)ntrepreneur roles, is called the Sprouting Founder because although he often founds an organization, he never really gets beyond the "sprouting" stage.

He is tremendously energetic – a self starter who sees his projects through to the end. Because he is task oriented, he is at his prime when the firm is small and growing. In the long run, however, the organization often outgrows his capabilities. When more formal controls are required, his style loses its effectiveness. It becomes dysfunctional, since he has no talent for (A)dministrating or (I)ntegrating, both of which are required for long-term organizational growth.

The Sprouting Founder is a creative risk taker, usually very outgoing. He sees farther than the Lone Ranger, since he has the (E) orientation, and unlike the Arsonist, he is goal oriented.

The Sprouting Founder starts his own fires and then tends them. He may have as many as 30 subordinates reporting to him, but basically he runs a one man show, with no time to (I)ntegrate or even delegate. His ideas are exciting. He knows how to (P)roduce results, and his subordinates simply try to emulate his style.

A manager with these strengths, plus competence at the (A) and (I) roles, would be a founder of an organization and potentially an excellent manager, But since the Sprouting Founder neither (A)dministers nor (I)ntegrates, the organization he leads cannot grow beyond his own managerial limitations, and furthermore, will usually crumble and disappear when he leaves or dies.

In addition to the Sprouting Founder, there is another type of (P-E-). This is the Mismatched Director of Professionals. He may be the director of an artistic organization, the medical director of a hospital, or a department chairman at an academic institution.

He is mismatched because he does not particularly care for (A)dministration or for (I)ntegrating people. He was probably promoted to this job because of his individual excellence as a (P)roducer,

(**E**)ntrepreneur, or both. But managing an organization requires more than the ability to dance, cure, or teach.

In the new position, he is frustrated and unhappy, and regards his job as a career mistake or a temporary assignment, the result of a huge personal sacrifice or the consequence of a self-destructive tendency on his part. He plays the martyr, constantly reminding himself and others how much he hates (**A**)dministration, how demoralizing it is, and how much he misses his true task in life. In actuality, he never returns to making art, practicing medicine, or doing research. He gets too hooked on the power game. He also appreciates the instant feedback that the (**A**)dministrative process provides, in contrast to the recognition he can expect from his professional activity, which may take forever to come, if it comes at all.

To be a good artist, one needs both the (**P**) and (**E**) orientations. (**A**)dministrative and (**I**)ntegrative abilities are far less important. Writers and painters, for example, have to come up with ideas, find a medium for communicating them, and see the process through to completion. They need (**E**) to create new things and (**P**) to see their projects through. The (**P**) orientation also permits them to disassociate themselves from their labor of love and let it go when it is completed. An artist who lacks (**P**) might never finish his work or let go of it even if he does get it completed. A person with (**P**) but no (**E**) could be a commercial artist: He produces but repeats himself constantly.

So for certain careers or jobs, having a (**P-E-**) style is not necessarily a disadvantage. However, for managers it is disastrous. And what often happens to (**P-E-**)s is that, because they are productive and ambitious, they are eventually promoted to a management job. A great actor may wish to be a director. The best doctor becomes the chief of staff. The most respected researcher is asked to head a university. Unfortunately, however, now their (**P**) and (**E**) will no longer be sufficient to fill the bill. An actor cannot direct unless he can (**I**)ntegrate an ensemble – (**I**). An artist who becomes an artistic director may be unable to handle the board of directors, plan systematically, or raise funds – (**A**).

The brilliant doctor who is appointed chief of staff may fight endlessly with his colleagues because he lacks (**I**). Because he is weak in (**A**), he may also fail to control the budget, hire the most qualified nurses, or supervise the handling of medical information.

In universities, alas, (**P-E-**) types often end up in leadership positions. Courses multiply – but the content remains unchanged even though the names are new. Academic cross fertilization within a department is often a mirage cherished only by aspiring new faculty members. (**P-E-**)s at universities are usually promoted to their positions because they published often and well. But can they (**I**)ntegrate other creative people? Can they (**A**)dminister? To be a good manager of professionals, one needs (**A**) and lots and lots of (**I**).

Both the Sprouting Founder and the Mismatched Director of Professionals fail as (**A**)dministrators, and therefore they tend to alienate the groups with whom they work. They are respected in their profession, but despised in their departments for the disorderly way they run things.

On the other hand, could an (**-A-I**) run a professional organization? Probably not, because his lack of (**P**) and (**E**) would cause him to be distrusted by the professionals he (**A**)dministrates for. Without the (**P**) and (**E**) traits that would have made him a skilled artist, doctor, teacher, or researcher, this mismanager would start out at a tremendous disadvantage in his department.

Still, the (**-A-I**) would probably do a better job as the leader of a professional organization than would the (**P-E-**): he would spend a good deal of time trying to please the professionals– (**I**) –and would provide them with an adequate support system – (**A**).

Ironically, however, although the (**P-E-**) would mismanage more seriously, he would also be more easily forgiven for his (**A**)dministrative failures because of his professional accomplishments. People would view him as a martyr who should "get the hell out of there" before "it gets to him."

Professional and high-tech organizations should have a (**PaEi**) as a professional director (artistic, medical, or academic, chief technical) and a (**pAeI**) as an (**A**)dministrative or business director. Both are needed.

Could a (**P-E-**) and an (**-A-I**) work together well? No; they probably would not be capable of working together at all, since each would be insensitive to and unappreciative of, the other's contributions. If the (**P-E-**) and the (**-A-I**) lack respect for each other, they are unlikely to cooperate with each other.

What is needed, then, is the ability to perform all the roles–particularly the (**I**) role – so they can appreciate each other. Thus, the most desirable of professional managers is the (**PaEI**) – if you can find one, because very few great professionals are capable of performing the (**I**) role. What usually makes them so successful is their (**E**) orientation, and (**E**)s are focused on making waves, not smoothing them. It is essential that the professional director have at least a modicum of ability in (**I**). Unfortunately, however, it often happens that an organization will single out the person whose (**E**) is largest for the position, and such a person's (**E**) has usually developed at the expense of his or her (**I**).

The Solo Developer, (PAE-)

This type of mismanager is a master at putting together a complex project and nurturing it until results are forthcoming. Because of his (**E**), he sees the big picture and can identify what results can be achieved. His (**P**) makes him results-oriented. His (**A**) is employed in creating a system to obtain the desired results. But without (**I**), he is just another example of a one man show.

In comparison to the Sprouting Founder, the Solo Developer's organization is capable of growing beyond his individual contributions, due to his (**A**). However, the organization will still experience difficulty when the Solo Developer leaves, because he was its only (**P**)roducer, (**A**)dministrator, and (**E**)ntrepreneur. His subordinates were mere followers. He did not build a team of other (**P**)roducers, (**A**)dministrators, and (**E**)ntrepreneurs who could maintain the previous rate of growth.

(**PAE-**)s could be great project managers in a very turbulent environment. They have great ideas about how to (**P**)roduce results and how to organize the system to achieve results, but they cannot create an environment in which their subordinates learn to generate such programs.

A variation of the Solo Developer is found in the construction indutry and in investment banking. The people who exemplify this variation have good ideas, know how to (**P**)roduce results, and can organize everything into a nice, neat package. But there is no continuity. The deal is made, and it must stand on its own. This person's departure will leave the organization in a difficult position.

THE DEMAGOGUE (- -EI)

This type of mismanager might be a convincing salesman or a run of the mill politician. Although he is creative and adaptive, his lack of (**P**) leaves him unconcerned about the consequences of his efforts.

As a politician, the Demagogue identifies the ideas that will appeal to his constituents and (**I**)ntegrates these into his own style in the form of promises. But he has no system for keeping these promises – no (**A**) – and no ability to deliver what he promises – no (**P**). He relies on his (**E**) capabilities to identify the messages (any messages) that will unify people.

If this manager had even a minimal competence in the (**P**) and (**A**) roles, he would be another kind of politician: A Statesman, (**paEI**). Without them, the Demagogue's aims are to generate excitement and interest and to rally support for himself. He makes promises irresponsibly. He does not know or care what the precise results will be. He worries about the results of the next election; what happens afterward will have to take care of itself.

The Demagogue differs from the Arsonist, (- **E** - -), in that he does not generate ideas solely to satisfy his ego. He listens to what people want, need, and expect. As an (**I**), he is able to detect social undercurrents. His (**E**) capability allows him to formulate a message that gives expression to those undercurrents. He makes the promises that people want to hear.

As a result, those who work for the Demagogue are so stirred up by his message that they will go all out for him, whereas the subordinates of the Arsonist do not follow him, although they claim that they do.

How does the Demagogue differ from the SuperFollower, (- - -I)? Because the SuperFollower must intervene personally in order to (I)ntegrate, he is capable of (I)ntegrating only a small group of people. By contrast, the (- - EI) can integrate by means of his ideas alone.

A subordinate of the Demagogue continually goes through a hot and cold emotional bath. While in the Demagogue's presence, the subordinate can find his ideas exciting and appropriate. But afterward, when he is finally alone he wonders where to begin or what to do. "What exactly did he want?" he may ask himself. The Demagogue had told the subordinate what he wanted to hear and had built up his aspirations to achieve *something* – but what was it?

In Mexico, such a leader is called an Alka Seltzer. He relieves you of your anxiety, but only for a few hours. Then you feel lousy again.

Bell calls this type of manager the Performer. Typically, the Performer is a smooth operator and a shrewd politician with outstanding social skills. He is a dynamic person who frequently does several things at a time. "To reach great successes," Bell suggests, "the Performer develops special talents in maneuvering others." These skills include pseudo-participation, making special deals, cooperating with other Performers, taking credit for successes, and parceling out compliments.[4]

Certain combinations of these flawed managers can be especially dangerous to an organization's health. For example, what would happen if the Demagogue manager had a Slave Driver (PA- -) subordinate?

The Demagogue's ideas and directions are very vague, whereas the Slave Driver wants to run a "tight ship"; thus he will figure out his own interpretation of what the Demagogue has said and proceed to do it or get it done. The Demagogue won't see any problems because he doesn't care what the Slave Driver does; like the Arsonist, the Demagogue simply enjoys the fact that someone is totally committed to his ideas. In the meantime, the uncreative Slave Driver may be cooking up a debacle.

One disastrous example of this combination of dysfunctional styles was the Watergate scandal. Richard Nixon was President, with H.R. (Bob) Haldeman and John Ehrlichman under him in charge of the White House staff. Nixon had ambitious visions (**E**) of statesmanship, breaking through the Silk Wall to China, and he was also an insecure person badly in need of support, (**I**), as was indicated by his bitterness toward the critical media. He had under him Slave Drivers or Taskmasters, such as Haldeman, who served him blindly. The result produced, I believe, a fantastic misunderstanding: Nixon, a (**paEI**), or (- - **EI**), the difference again is one of degree, not of essence, gave directions that may have been too general, which were then interpreted and implemented by Haldeman, in detail, without any real vision or ethical considerations.[5]

Thus, the partnership of a (**PA- -**) and an (- - **EI**) is potentially dangerous. On the other hand, the combination of a (**PaEi**) and a (**pAeI**) could work well, as long as the (**pAeI**) does not mind being in the supportive role. Hospitals, operas, theaters, and universities are often run by such partnerships.

Our next combined style of mismanagement occurs when the already enthusiastic Demagogue also has the ability to organize.

THE FALSE LEADER, (- AEI)

This manager generates ideas, (**I**)ntegrates people behind those ideas, and establishes a system to implement them.

However, the False Leader's system does not (**P**)roduce results. People follow the False Leader and carry out their assigned tasks, but in the long run their beliefs are shattered because what is promised never materializes. The False Leader *does* organize, he *does* (**I**)ntegrate his staff to carry out a mission, but the activities he organizes ultimately fail.

(**P**) skills can easily be misplaced. When a manager gets carried away with too much power, he risks losing the social judgment that is a necessary component for (**P**). Or he might become so confident of his own infallibility that he forgets that without knowledge, (**P**) is fruitless. Hitler failed spectacularly in this way, ignoring information – particularly unhappy information – from the field.

A common industrial example of a False Leader is the manager who is brought in to save a failing company. People have unrealistic expectations of him, perhaps looking up to him as a savior. He may be very achievement-oriented, but if he has not yet learned the technology of his new company – its market, what "makes it tick"–his (**P**) will be weak and the ability to achieve his goals will be compromised. Such a person may be a great (**E**)ntrepreneur, (**A**)dministrator, and (**I**)ntegrator, but without the technical know-how necessary for (**P**), he will not understand what is needed.

There are endless examples in industry of this type of manager: eager to succeed, good (**A**)dministrators, (**E**)ntrepreneurs, and (**I**)ntegrators – but ignorant of the necessary technical know-how and without the time they need to acquire it. These managers are incapable of (**P**)roducing results.

In his book *Top Management Planning*[6], George Steiner describes what happened to the Winchester Company in the 1920s and '30s, when the company president filled key positions by appointing managers who had no previous experience in the field. It's an old story, but if you change the names and add some zeros, you'll find that the circumstances match any number of more recent corporate fiascos.

Winchester added about a thousand new products in 1923-24. Unfortunately, the new products competed with Winchester's bread and butter items, so to improve sales the company decided to merge with its major competitor. Suddenly, Winchester salesmen had to sell products that they had previously criticized. The results? Sales declined from $18 million in 1923 to $7 million in 1931.

Obviously, it is not enough to innovate and change. A manager must have intimate knowledge of the field in which he innovates in order to make competent judgments. Change for the sake of change can have disastrous effects.

Our next combined style of mismanagement combines creative (**E**) with control oriented (**A**), but lacks the (**P**) and (**I**) orientations. This gives us a unique style of mismanager, whom I call the Pain in the Neck.

THE PAIN IN THE NECK, (- A E -)

The Pain in the Neck is full of suggestions for innovation and change, and wants to control in detail all aspects of what is being done. Furthermore, he is insensitive to other people and incapable of (**I**)ntegrating their ideas into a cohesive whole.

He behaves somewhat like a schizophrenic. He is ridden with internal tensions. He needs to control conflicts with his desire to change things. He gets very excited about perceived opportunities, while at the same time he can't help worrying about the risks involved and foreseeing all the complications that might threaten his ultimate success.

With such ambivalence and internal conflicts it is not strange that his (**P**) orientation is minimal if not non-existent.

The Pain in the Neck is habitually ambivalent and frustrated with his own "impotence." This makes him seem brooding, dissatisfied, unfriendly, and unsupportive. In meetings he is perverse, always arguing on the other side of the fence: If the discussion concerns details of operational control, for example, he will bring up the "big picture" and complain that "we are not adapting to the changing needs of our markets." If the discussion is about long-term future trends, he will focus on all the barriers to change and insist that it is dangerous to proceed.

The (-**AE**-)'s tendency to play devil's advocate makes him controversial and unpopular, particularly because he makes it impossible to be on the same side that he is on.

If the Pain in the Neck had even a modicum of (**P**) orientation, he would be a good problem-solver; he could take a complex problem (**E**) and structure it so that it was controllable (**A**) and (**P**)roduced results (**P**). However, without (**I**), he still could not be a consultant. At best, a (**pAE-**) can be a competent staff person. Let him write reports. Do not let him manage anything.

The Pain in the Neck (**-AE-**) resembles Bell's Attacker[7], who habitually rebels against authority and social custom. This is the (**E**) orientation in him. The Attacker also tends to be a nitpicker: given a project, he expends a great deal of energy finding mistakes and problems with it. That is his (**A**) orientation. Paradoxically, however, he avoids responsibility by acting uncommitted and failing to show interest in projects. This demonstrates his lack of (**P**). Since he has no (**I**) either, he projects his internal conflicts onto others and thus alienates them.

To shield himself from his environment, the Attacker will form a group of Attackers around him. This group will develop cynical perspectives and reinforce these perspectives in one another. They will attack anything and everything that is presented to them. In one situation, they will argue that a certain task needs to be limited and monitored, exhibiting their (**A**). In another situation they will argue that not enough is being done, demonstrating their (**E**): "You should always be moving."

Whatever approach someone takes, the Attacker goes to work to present the other side. And since he often changes his mind, he is constantly at odds with himself. This makes him a bitter, bitchy, hypercritical, frustrated Pain in the Neck! As a consultant, the (**- AE -**) is dangerous: he will offer ideas on how to change a system to promote better control, but he fails to consider the need for teamwork, and he has only a primitive grasp of what the system is for.

THE CHARISMATIC GURU, (P-EI)

An effective leader creates new directions (**E**), motivates his fellow workers (**I**), and gets consistently successful results (**P**) by systematizing the process (**A**). The Charismatic Guru, in contrast, creates these results with his charisma.

Unlike the Demagogue, the Guru does (**P**)roduce results. He also identifies the big picture, for both the short and the long-term. He (**I**)ntegrates people and sets out to make effective changes. He worries about the next generation, not necessarily the next election.

The Charismatic Guru's creativity is results oriented. He has a commitment to certain goals, and he focuses his (**E**)ntrepreneurship on them. Furthermore, he is a capable persuader, able to communicate his ideas in a way that (**I**)ntegrates, focuses, and inspires people. That is what makes him a Guru.

But he lacks (**A**), which means he won't systematize and probably won't even grasp the importance of process. It is the Guru's personal style that his followers admire; when he leaves the company or dies, his staff must quickly systematize and ritualize his teachings, or his influence will disappear.

One of the (**P-EI**)s I analyzed was charismatic, (**P**)roduced results, and was head and shoulders above his peers. But when he died his organization had difficulty surviving because it had not been organized for effectiveness and efficiency. To a large degree, its past achievements had been dependent upon the personal style of its late leader. His techniques had not been systematized; thus, the company was like a ship that had lost its navigator.

The Charismatic Guru is a kind of False Leader, in the sense that he appears to be the perfect manager but does not come through in the long run. He compensates for his lack of (**A**) with his charisma, but once he is gone, the latent (**A**) deficiency becomes fully obvious. The (**I**)ntegration he achieved will soon erode without him. Results will diminish, and eventually the (**E**) he bequeathed will have no opportunity to express itself.

Thus, charismatic leadership can also be a type of mismanagement, because the life span of organizations is, or should be, longer than that of any individual. If an organization's success depends on one individual, in the long run the organization will not survive.

NOTES

1. Theodore H. White: *Breach of Faith* (New York: Atheneum, 1975), p. 105.

2. Bell, Gerald: *The Achievers* (Chapel Hill, N.C.: Preston Hill, 1973), ch. 2.

3. "Ranger Diplomacy of Mr. Kissinger," *New York Times*, Dec. 4, 1976, p. 13.

4. Bell, op. cit., ch. 6.

5. Bob Haldeman was a highly respected associate of Adizes Institute until his death. He and I spent many hours trying to analyze what combination of circumstances caused the Watergate fiasco, which led to the impeachment of the president of the United States. Bob is sorely missed.

6. George Albert Steiner: *Top Management Planning* (New York: Macmillan, 1969).

7. Bell, op. cit., ch. 3.

Test Yourself

QUIZ NO. 1

A Review of Roles and Styles

Fill in the blank with (**P**), (**A**), (**E**) or (**I**), depending on which style is best characterized by each statement.

(__) 1. He likes subordinates to emulate his own ways of accomplishing tasks.

(__) 2. He knows most of the standard operating procedures by heart.

(__) 3. He changes direction without warning.

(__) 4. He often says, "If I can do it, you should be able to do it too."

(__) 5. He tries to find out which way the political wind is blowing within the organization, and then he tries to follow in that direction.

(__) 6. He spreads himself too thin.

(__) 6a. He spreads others too thin.

(__) 7. He manages largely by writing directives.

(__) 8. He believes that we should not worry too much about long-term planning. He says, "If we don't achieve results today there might be no tomorrow."

(__) 9. He thinks that anyone who can't do a job is an "academician."

(__) 10. The best thing to do is avoid him because he always has a new job for you to do in spite of the fact that you are already occupied.

(__) 11. His main concern is always to achieve a consensus within the organization.

(__) 12. He has little sense of what people are capable of accomplishing.

(__) 13. He becomes very excited about his own ideas.

(__) 14. He prefers to get results working alone.

(__) 15. He considers departmental tasks his own personal responsibility.

(__) 16. He does not care about achieving anything beyond controlling the organization's behavior.

(__) 17. He delegates new responsibilities and duties before the old ones have been accomplished.

(__) 18. He always has many reasons at hand to show why change should not be made.

(__) 19. He expects that success should have been achieved already.

(__) 20. He likes to see the organization kept busy, regardless of the results they are producing.

(__) 21. He tries to accomplish tasks by himself.

(__) 22. If there is a power struggle going on among members of the organization, he will not intervene until it is already resolved one way or the other.

(__) 23. His subordinates try to look busy in order not to receive additional tasks.

(__) 24. He thinks that no one can do things as well as he can.

(__) 25. He takes risks.

(__) 26. He cares more about how things are done than about what is being done.

(__) 27. He becomes upset when tasks are not accomplished even though he had given his subordinates the impression that those tasks had been abandoned.

(__) 28. He relies on expeditors, i.e., assistants who do not have a permanent role but who carry out specific assignments that he gives them.

(__) 29. His subordinates accept assignments but do not carry them out because they are not sure if he really means what he is asking them to do.

(__) 30. Cliques and special interest groups flourish under his management.

(__) 31. He changes his mind frequently.

(__) 32. He does not delegate enough.

(__) 33. He does not follow up on assignments on a regular basis.

Answers	1. P	9. P	18. A	27. E
0-3 wrong = Excellent	2. A	10. E	19. E	28. P
4-6 wrong = Good	3. E	11. I	20. E	29. E
7-9 wrong = Fair	4. P	12. E	21. P	30. I
10 or more wrong: Go back	5. I	13. E	22. I	31. E
and read Chapters 1-9 again.	6. P	14. P	23. E	32. P
	6a.E	15. P	24. P	33. E
	7. A	16. A	25. E	34. E
	8. P	17. E	26. A	35. E
				36. P

QUIZ NO. 2

Quotes Test for Styles

The following are quotes said by some famous people. Can you match them with a management style?[1]

(__) 1. "Between two living beings, harmony is never given. It has to be worked on again and again."– advertising for the *World Equestrian Games*, Jerez, September 10-22,

(__) 2. "I like it, I do it. That's my code."–*Alan Denlon*

(__) 3. "Be not afraid of going slowly; be only afraid of standing still."–*Chinese proverb*

(__) 4. "Per ardua ad astra." ("By striving we reach the stars.") – *Royal Air Force motto*

(__) 5. "It is far easier to begin a task than to finish it."–*Titus Maccius Plautus*

(__) 6. "If it isn't happening, make it happen."–*David Hemmings*

(__) 7. "All that I can, I will."–*French saying*

(__) 8. "There is no penalty for overachievement."– *George William Miller*

(__) 9. "The only people who never fail are those who never try."– *Ilka Chase*

(__) 10. "Act as if it were impossible to fail."– *Dorothea Brande*

(__) 11. "Man needs difficulties; they are necessary for health."– *Carl Jung*

(__) 12. "The road to success is always under construction."– *Arnold Palmer*

(__) 13. "If you're going to be thinking anyway, you might as well think big."– *Donald Trump*

(__) 14. "No one knows what is in him till he tries, and many would never try if they were not forced to."– *Basil W. Maturin*

(__) 15. "Just keep going. Everybody gets better if they keep at it."– *Ted Williams*

(__) 16. "You see things; and you say, 'Why?' But I dream things that never were; and I say, 'Why not?'"– *George Bernard Shaw*

(__) 17. "Winning is living. Every time you win, you're reborn. When you lose, you die a little."– *George Allen*

(__) 18. "Sweat is the cologne of accomplishment."– *Heywood Hale Brown*

(__) 19. "When you reach the top, that's when the climb begins."– *Michael Caine*

(__) 20. "We strain hardest for things which are almost but not quite within our reach."– *Frederick W. Faber*

(__) 21. "The only place where success comes before work is in a dictionary."– *Vidal Sassoon*

(__) 22. "It ain't over till it's over."– *Yogi Berra*

(__) 23. "Just get out there and do what you've got to do."– *Anonymous*

Here is what I think :

1. (I)	7. (P)	14. (E then P)	21. (P)
2. (PE)	8. (P)	15. (P)	22. (P)
3. (pA)	9. (E)	16. (E)	23. (P)
4. (PE)	10. (E)	17. (E)	
5. (E)	11. (P)	18. (P)	
6. (E)	12. (A)	19. (E)	
	13. (E)	20. (E)	

To test your style or the style of your colleagues more precisely and to differentiate between the style you have, the style you would like to have, and the style your job calls for, go to the Adizes Institute website: http://www.adizes.com/tools.html

Click on "Management Style Indicator."

For a free and fast preliminary test to indicate your style, go to Managementvitality.com.

NOTES

1. From "Go For It! A Photographic Celebration" by Hulton Getty; *Mpq Creative, Editor* (New York: William Morrow, $10).

Afterword

We are all different, thank God. This enables us to learn from others. It is painful, true. But you do not learn from similarities alone. It is the complementary differences that teach you.

Each one of us has a style with its specific strengths and weaknesses. We fulfill certain roles, some well, some badly, roles that the organization needs.

We need each other, not in spite of but because of our differences, if our marriages, organizations, communities, and societies are going to be healthy in the short and long run.

The purpose of this book was to provide tools that classify which roles people perform and how their style manifests itself. In Part 3 of this series, *Leading the Leaders - Enrich Your Style of Management and Handle People Whose Style is Different from Yours*, I offer specific prescriptions for each style, based on my research and experience in the field working with all four types, on how to communicate, manage, be managed, or co-manage with those we need, those who complement us.

If you proceed to that book you can skip the first chapters, which summarize the contents of this book. If you have time, however, I recommend reading them anyway, because those chapters will reinforce and remind you of what you have learned so far, and there is always something new to learn.

And I repeat my request from the Preface: Anyone who wants to disagree with what I have said so far, or has an insight, or an anecdote, or a joke, or a cartoon that relates to the content of this book, is welcome to get in touch with me at ichak@adizes.com.

Ichak Kalderon Adizes
Santa Barbara, California

Bibliography

Abravanel, E. and King, E.: *Dr. Abravanel's Body Type Program for Health, Fitness and Nutrition* (New York: Bantam Books, Inc. 1985).

Adizes, Ichak: *How to Solve the Mismanagement Crisis* (Santa Monica, Calif.: Adizes Institute, Inc., 1979).

Adizes, Ichak: *Industrial Democracy, Yugoslav Style: The Effect of Decentralization on Organizational Behavior* (New York: Free Press, 1971; reprinted by MDOR Institute, 1977, paper).

Adizes, Ichak: *Managing Corporate Lifecycles* (Paramus, N.J.: Prentice Hall Press, 1999).

Adizes, Ichak: *Managing the Performing Arts Organization: Founding Principles in the Management of the Arts* (Santa Monica, Calif.: The Adizes Institute, 1999).

Adizes, Ichak: *Mastering Change: The Power of Mutual Trust and Respect* (Santa Barbara, Calif.: Adizes Institute Publications, 1992).

Alessandra, A. and Wexler, P.: *Non-Manipulative Selling* (San Diego: Courseware, Inc., 1979).

Bell, Gerald: *The Achievers* (Chapel Hill, N.C.: Preston Hill, 1973).

Bennett, E.: *What Jung Really Said* (New York: Schocken Books, 1967).

Bennett, J.: *Enneagram Studies* (York Beach: Samuel Weiser, Inc., 1983).

Berliner, Joseph S.: *Factory and Manager in the USSR* (Cambridge, Mass.: Harvard University Press, 1957).

Berne, Eric: *Games People Play* (New York: Ballantine, 1996, revised edition).

Blake, Robert, and Mouton, Jane: *The Managerial Grid* (Houston: Gulf Publishing, 1964).

Blau, Peter M.: *The Dynamics of Bureaucracy* (Chicago: University of Chicago Press, 1956).

Bolton, R. and Bolton, D.: *People Styles at Work* (New York: American Management Association, 1996).

Bolton, R. and Bolton, D.: *Social Style/Management Style* (New York: American Management Association, 1984).

Choiniere, R., and Keirsey, D.: *Presidential Temperament* (Del Mar: Prometheus Nemesis Book Company, 1992).

Drucker, Peter F.: *Management: Tasks, Responsibilities, Practices* (New York: Harper & Row, 1973).

Fieve, Ronald R.: *Moodswing: Dr. Fieve on Depression* (New York: William Morrow and Co., 1989).

Francis, Roy G., and Stone, Robert C.: *Service and Procedure in Bureaucracy: A Case Study* (Minneapolis: University of Minnesota Press, 1956).

Fraser, J.: *The Chinese Portrait of a People* (Glasgow: William Collins Sons & Co. Ltd., 1981).

Gordon, Dr. T.: *L.E.T. Leadership Effectiveness Training* (Wyden Books, 1977).

Halberstam, D.: *The Best and the Brightest* (London: Pan Books Ltd., 1972).

Hartman, T.: *The Color Code* (Taylor Don Hartman, 1987).

Herrmann, N.: *The Creative Brain* (Lake Lure: Brain Books, 1990).

Keirsey, D. and Bates, M.: *Please Understand Me* (Del Mar: Prometheus Nemesis Book Company, 1984).

Lear, F.: *The Second Seduction* (New York: Alfred A. Knopf, 1992).

Lowen, A.: *Depression and the Body* (New York: Penguin Books, 1981).

Lowen, A.: *The Language of the Body* (New York: Macmillan Publishing Co., Inc., 1979).

March, James G., and Herbert Simon: *Organizations* (New York, London: John Wiley & Sons, 1958).

Mottram, V.: *The Physical Basis of Personality* (Baltimore: Penguin Books, 1960).

Parkinson, C. Northcote: *Parkinson's Law: The Pursuit of Progress* (London: John Murray, 1958).

Peter, Laurence J., and Hull, Raymond: *The Peter Principle: Why Things Always Go Wrong* (New York: William Morrow & Co., 1969).

Rothchild, J.: *Going for Broke: How Robert Campeau Bankrupted the Retail Industry, Jolted the Junk Bond Market and Brought the Booming Eighties to a Crashing Halt* (New York: Simon & Schuster, 1991).

Schumpeter, Joseph: *Business Cycles* (New York: McGraw Hill, 1939).

Soros, George; Wien, Byron; and Koenen, Krisztina: *Soros on Soros: Staying Ahead of the Curve* (New York: John Wiley & Sons, 1995).

George Albert Steiner: *Top Management Planning* (New York: Macmillan, 1969).

Storm, H.: *Seven Arrows* (New York: Harper & Row, 1972).

Sundberg, N.: *Assessment of Persons* (New Jersey: Prentice-Hall, 1977).

Waldo, Dwight, ed., *Ideas and Issues in Public Administration* (New York: McGraw Hill, 1963).

Woodward, Joan: *Industrial Organization: Theory and Practice* (New York: Oxford University Press, 1965).

Additional Works by the Author

(All available from Adizes Institute at www.adizes.com)

BOOKS

Adizes, I.: *Industrial Democracy Yugoslav Style*. New York: Free Press, 1971.

Adizes, I. and Mann-Borgese, Elisabeth, eds.: *Self-Management: New Dimensions to Democracy*. Santa Barbara, CA: ABC/CLIO, 1975.

Adizes, I.: *How to Solve the Mismanagement Crisis*. 2nd printing. Santa Barbara: Adizes Institute Publications, 1980. (First printing, New York: Dow Jones Irwin, 1979.)

Adizes, I.: *Corporate Lifecycles: How and Why Corporations Grow and Die and What to do about It*. Englewood Cliffs, NJ: Prentice Hall, 1988.

Adizes, I.: *Mastering Change: The Power of Mutual Trust and Respect in Personal Life, Family, Business and Society*. Santa Barbara: Adizes Institute Publications, 1993.

Adizes, I.: *The Pursuit of Prime*. First printing, Santa Monica, CA: Knowledge Exchange, 1996.

Adizes, I.: *Managing the Performing Arts Organization*. Forthcoming publication. Santa Barbara: Adizes Institute Publications, 1999.

Adizes, I.: *Managing Corporate Lifecycles: An updated and expanded look at the Corporate Lifecycles*. First printing, Paramus, NJ: Prentice Hall Press, 1999.

Adizes, I.: *The Ideal Executive, Why You Cannot Be One and What to Do about It*. The Adizes Institute Publications, 2004.

Adizes, I.: *Leading the Leaders, How to Enrich Your Style of Management and Handle People whose Style is Different from Yours*. The Adizes Institute Publications, 2004.

ARTICLES

Adizes, I. "The Role of Management in Democratic (Communal) Organizational Structures." *Annals of Public and Cooperative Economy.* Quarterly review of CIRIEC. Brussels: CIRIEC, No. 424 (1971): 399–420.

Adizes, I. "Administering for the Arts: Introduction and Overview." *California Management Review* 15,2 (1972): 99–103.

Adizes, I. "Boards of Directors in the Performing Arts: A Managerial Analysis." *California Management Review* 15, 2 (1972): 109 117.

Adizes, I. "Economic Changes in Yugoslavia." *East Europe* 21, 10 (1972): 8–16.

Adizes, I. "Management in Der Demokratischen Organisationen." *Annalen der Gemeinwirtschaft* 41 (Januar-Marz, 1972).

Adizes, I. "Samoupravljanje Kao Drustveni Cilj i Organizacijski Proces - [Self-Management as a Social Goal and an Organizational Process."] *Socijalizam* 11, 12 (1972): 1324–1333.

Adizes, I. "Uloga Rukovodjenja u Demokratskim Organizacionim Strukturama." [Serbo-Croatian translation of "The Role of Management in Democratic Organizational Structures"]. *Moderna Organizacija* 6 (1972): 937–951.

Adizes, I. "Uloga Vodstva v Demokraticnih (Skupnostnih) Organizacijskih Strukturah." ["The Role of Management in Democratic Organization"] *Moderna Organizacija* 6 (1972): 437–451.

Adizes, I. and Weston, F. "Comparative Models of Social Responsibility." *Journal of the Academy of Management* 16, 1 (1973): 112–129. Reprinted in F. Luthans and R.M. Hodgetts, *Social Issues in Business.* 2nd ed. New York: Macmillan, 1974.

Adizes, I. "Gerencia y Estructuras Comunales (I)." "The Role of Management in Democratic Organization" *Gerencia.* Instituto Peruano de Administracion de Empresas (IPAE) Lima, Peru, (Noviembre/Diciembre, 1976): 23–76. Adizes, I. "On Conflict Resolution and an Organizational Definition of Self-Management" in *Participation and Self-Management*, Volume 5 "Social

System and Participation," 1–73. First International Sociological Conference on Participation and Self-Management. Zagreb, Yugoslavia (1973).

Adizes, I. "Le Role de la Direction Dans une Communante Organisée Sûr une Base Democratique." "The Role of Management in Democratic Organization" *Les Annales De L'Economie Collective* 1 (Jan.-Mars, 1973): 83–109.

Adizes, I. and McWhinney, W. "Arts, Society and Administration: The Role and Training of Arts Administrators, Arts and Society." *Arts and Society*, 10, 3 (1974): 40–50.

Adizes, I. "Gerencia y Estructuras Comunales (II) Management and Communal Structures" *Gerencia*, IPAE (January/February, 1974): 36–43.

Adizes, I. "Relaciones Organizativas en la Empresa Autogestionaria [The Self-Managed Enterprise]." *Apuntes* 1, 2 (1974): 21–30.

Blame, M. and Adizes, I. "Parkview Symphony." In *Business Policy: Strategy Formation and Management Action*, ed. W. Glueck, 366–374. 2nd ed. New York: McGraw-Hill, 1974.

Adizes, I. "Autogestion y Naciones en Dsarollo [Self-Management in Developing Nations]." *Apuntes* 4 (1975): 106–122.

Adizes, I. "The Cost of Being an Artist: An Argument for the Public Support of the Arts." *California Management Review* 17 (Summer, 1975): 80–84.

Adizes, I. "Mas Alla del 'Principio de Peter': una Tipologia de Estilos de Incompetencis Gerencial." *Instituto de Administracion Cientifica de las Empresas* (lACE). Monterrey, Mexico (1975).

Adizes, I. "Mismanagement Styles." *California Management Review* 19, 2 (1976): 5–20.

Adizes, I. "Seattle Opera Association." *Business Policy: Strategy Formation and Management Action*, ed. W. Glueck, 610–634. 2nd ed. New York: McGraw-Hill, 1976.

Adizes, I. and Zukin, P. "A Management Approach to Health Planning in Developing Countries." *Health Care Management Review* 2, 1 (1977): 19–37.

Adizes, I. "Industrial Democracy and Codetermination." *Ency-*

clopedia of Professional Management. New York: McGraw-Hill, 1978.

Zupanov, J. and Adizes, I., "Labor Relations in Yugoslavia." Handbook of Contemporary Developments in *World Industrial Relations*, ed. A. Blum. Westwood, CT: Greenwood Press, 1978.

Adizes, I. "Mismanagement." *Affarsekonomi Management. Stockholm*, Sweden, 1978.

Adizes, I. "Organizational Passages: Tools for Diagnosis and Therapy of Organizational Behavior." *Organizational Dynamics* 8, 3 (Summer, 1979): 28–46.

Adizes, I. and Turban, E., "An Innovative Approach to Group Decision Making." *Personnel*, 62,4 (1985): 45–49.

Adizes, I. "Back to Basics: Mutual Trust and Respect and Productivity." *Executive Excellence*, 10, 10 (1993): 11–13.

Adizes, I. "Managing: The Business of Mutual Trust and Respect." *Manage* 45, 1 (1993): 26–28.

Adizes, I. "Twelve Tips on Keeping Your Growing Business at Prime." *Manage* 44,3 (1993): 14–17.

Adizes, I. "Corporate Lifecycles: Entrepreneurship and Integration." In *Management and Entrepreneurship*, the English version, ed. I. Vaji, 168 172. Vol. II. Centar za Management i Marketing, University of Zagreb: Zagreb University Press, 1994.

Adizes, I. "How to Convert a Committee into a Team." *Successful Meetings* 43, 2 (1994): 115–118.

Adizes, I. "Integrating Innovation." *Executive Excellence.* 11, 11 (1994): 12–13.

Adizes, I. "Keeping the Fires Burning [about TQM]." *Manage* 46, 1 (1994): 12 16.

Adizes, I. "Information Superhighway: Overloading Human Potential." *Executive Excellence* 12, 4 (1995): 15.

Adizes, I. "What Comes First? Strategy or Structure?" *Executive Excellence* 2, 9 (1995): 20.

Adizes, I. "Eight Myths [about management]: Getting Right the People Dimension of Business." *Executive Excellence* 14, 9 (1997): 20.

Adizes, I. "Five Myths about Management in the 1990s." *Manage* 48 (July, 1997): 30 32.

Adizes, I. "Looking for Mr./Ms. Perfect: The Search for the Right Professional Manager in a Growing Company. *Progress* 2, 1 (1998): 14–15.

Adizes, I. "Self-Esteem: Who Cares?" *The Adizes Institute Journal of Organizational Transformation* 1, 1 (1998): 7–16.

Working Papers

Adizes, I. Establishing a Program for Arts Administration: Summary of the UCLA Conference and a Report on Implementation. In the *Management in the Arts Research Program Publication Series*, Publication 1. Division of Research, GSM. Los Angeles: UCLA, 1969.

Adizes, I. "The Roles of Art in Post-Industrial Society." Presented at the *Center for the Study of Democratic Institutions.* Santa Barbara, CA: January, 1973.

Adizes, I. "Administering for the Arts: Problems in Practice." *Management in the Arts Program Research Papers*, #15. GSM. Los Angeles: UCLA, October, 1971.

Adizes, I. "A New Framework for Management Theory." Santa Barbara: The Adizes Institute, June, 1987.

Adizes, I. and Haldeman, H.R. "Why Gorbachev Might Fail." Santa Barbara: The Adizes Institute, January, 1988.

Adizes, I. "The Common Principles of Managing Oneself, a Family, a Corporation or a Society." Santa Barbara: The Adizes Institute, September, 1990.

VIDEO

Adizes, I. (1984). *The Adizes Program in Video.* Santa Barbara: The Adizes Institute.

Adizes, I. *Program A: Overview of the Adizes Process of Management.* Set of 3 videotapes. Santa Barbara: Adizes Institute Publications, 1993

The Adizes Process of Management. 55 min.

The Adizes Program. Questions and Answers #1

The Adizes Program. Questions and Answers # 2

Adizes I. *Program B: The Management Process.* Set of 4 videotapes. Santa Barbara: Adizes Institute Publications, 1993

The Roles of Management. 28 min.

Mismanagement Styles. 41 min.

The Structural Causes of Deadwood. 38 min.

What is a Good Manager? 41 min.

Adizes I. *Program C: Organizational Lifecycles.* Set of 4 videotapes. Santa Barbara: Adizes Institute Publications, 1993

The Growth Phases of Organizational Lifecycles. 39 min.

The Aging Phases of Organizational Lifecycles. 38 min.

Analysis of Lifecycles. 52 min.

Treating the Growing and Aging Problems of Organizations. 56 min.

Adizes, I. *Program D: Decision Making and Implementation.* Set of 2 videotapes. Santa Barbara: Adizes Institute Publications, 1993.

CAPI: Predicting Managerial Effectiveness. 45 min.

The Adizes Process of Decision Making. 49 min.

Adizes, I. *From Entrepreneurship to Professional Management.* Speech to the Council of Growing Companies. Santa Barbara: Adizes Institute Publications, 1993.

Adizes, I. *The Young Company's Lifecycle: Are You Ready for the Future?* Keynote Address to the Inc. 500 Awards. Santa Barbara: Adizes Institute Publications, 1996.

AUDIO

Adizes, I. *Analysis of Management.* 6 audio cassettes. Santa Barbara: Adizes Institute Publications, 1988.

Adizes, I. *Analysis of Lifecycles.* 6 audio cassettes. Santa Barbara: Adizes Institute Publications, 1989.

CD

Caric, N., Horvat, Z. and Vukic, B. *The Adizes Program: An Interactive Compilation of the Writings of Dr. Ichak Adizes and the Programs of the Adizes Institute*. Santa Barbara: Adizes Institute Publications, 1998.

ABOUT THE ADIZES INSTITUTE

The Adizes Institute provides organizations worldwide with the managerial resources to achieve extraordinary results while developing and nurturing a constructive, cooperative organizational culture.

Since its establishment in 1975, the Adizes Institute has served hundreds of organizations worldwide, from fledging companies to Fortune 100s, not-for-profit organizations, and governments. Through its network of international locations, the Adizes Institute has provided services to organizations in 45 countries.

The Adizes Institute is the research, publishing, licensing, training, and certification arm for the Adizes® methodology. The Adizes® methodology, developed over the past 35 years by Dr. Ichak Adizes, is a highly evolved proprietary, structured, pragmatic system for accelerating organizational change.

The Adizes Institute is closely associated with the Adizes Graduate School that grants master's and doctoral degrees in the study of Leadership and Change.